"Alice Potter has done it again! Her *Positive Thinker's Ten Commandments* is an excellent tool for super-busy executives who wish to enhance their thinking and their bottom line."

—AMY BERGER, author of
The Twenty Year Itch

"Alice Potter sprinkles her writing liberally with stories and thought-provoking quotes that delight and intrigue."

—SUSAN PAGE, author of
*How One of You Can Bring
the Two of You Together*

"Alice Potter has given us not only a decalogue of delight, but of health and success, too. Here are ten commandments that are fun to keep!"

—DAVID KUNDTZ, author of
Stopping and *Everyday Serenity*

Berkley Books by Alice Potter

THE POSITIVE THINKER
PUTTING THE POSITIVE THINKER TO WORK
THE POSITIVE THINKER'S 10 COMMANDMENTS
I CAN DO THAT!

The Positive Thinker's 10 Commandments

For a Happier, Healthier, More Successful You

ALICE POTTER

Illustrations by Elena Facciola

BERKLEY BOOKS, NEW YORK

THE POSITIVE THINKER'S 10 COMMANDMENTS: FOR A HAPPIER, HEALTHIER, MORE SUCCESSFUL YOU

A Berkley Book / published by arrangement with
the author

PRINTING HISTORY
Berkley edition / January 2001

The Penguin Putnam Inc. World Wide Web site address is
http://www.penguinputnam.com

ISBN: 0-425-17817-X

BERKLEY®
Berkley Books are published by The Berkley Publishing Group,
a division of Penguin Putnam Inc.,
375 Hudson Street, New York, New York 10014.
BERKLEY and the "B" design
are trademarks belonging to Penguin Putnam Inc.

PRINTED IN THE UNITED STATES OF AMERICA

10 9 8 7 6 5 4 3 2 1

To Mark

A fine son
A fabulous father

CONTENTS

Acknowledgments ix

Introduction xi

The Commandments

I Take Care of Your Body 1

II Expand Your Mind 57

III Nurture Your Spirit 91

IV Be Responsible and
Trustworthy in All Ways 115

V Honor Your Relationships 143

VI Live Up to Your Potential
and Do Whatever It Takes 173

VII Communicate Effectively
in All Areas of Life 199

VIII Be Tolerant and Compassionate—
Develop Empathy and Forgive 225

IX Love One Another 247

X Have Fun—Enjoy—
Live Life to the Fullest 275

Acknowledgments

I am forever in debt to my publishing company, The Berkley Publishing Group, a division of Penguin Putnam Inc., for allowing me to write under their imprint, and to my editors, Hillary Cige, who launched this project, and Christine Zika, who saw me through the rough spots and final phases. Thank you, thank you.

When writing a book, it is impossible to thank all of the people who helped with the process from conception to completion. Since I am a people person, I always rely on friends and colleagues when involved in a project; I have seldom been let down.

In response to my pleas for input, once again, many friends and colleagues readily responded with personal stories and suggestions. I offer my sincere thanks and grateful appreciation to the following generous contributors: Dolores Tversky, Marty Nemko, Art Sasser, Dan Nelson, John Gill Wright, Annette Martin, Barbara Witt, Fern Barker, Craig Harrison, Evalee Harrison, Roger and Victoria Smith, and Capt. Gerald Coffee.

Extra special thanks go to those whom I know I can count on without fail and who have always always gone the extra mile for me: Fred Schiavo, Michael Lee, Allen

Klein, Mary McNeill, Amy Berger, my fabulous illustrator and dear friend, Elena Facciola, and my prolific pen pals: Paul Christmann and Bob Jackson.

And to all my dear friends—and you know who you are—who gave me unconditional love, encouragement, affection, and much needed support during a very difficult time in my life, I give you my undying love in return.

Last but not least, I thank Charlie, my dear canine companion who guards me, keeps me sane, and whose constant presence is a joy.

Thank you. I love you all.

Introduction

The life which is unexamined is not worth living.

—PLATO

WHO am I to undertake the auspicious task of writing a book that dares to outline the Ten Commandments of life that promise a happier, healthier, more successful you—and how do I dare to have the audacity to even attempt such an undertaking?

The answers to these questions, my dear reader, is why this book has been tardy in its conception and slow in its completion.

The fact is that I do not have the answers, I only have ongoing questions. And I have an unquenchable desire to learn, to know, and to understand. To *examine,* as Plato said. For years I've heard that if you want to learn, know, or understand something, you must teach it. That makes sense to me because if you truly want to learn, know, and understand, you'll do whatever it takes to do so. You'll read, research, talk, and explore in your quest for answers and knowledge. And, ultimately, you'll teach it.

He who can, does. He who cannot, teaches.

—GEORGE BERNARD SHAW

Writing this book is my method of teaching in order to more fully learn, know, and understand; to *examine* life.

And so, over the past couple of decades, I've become a quest-for-knowledge self-help junkie. My bookshelves are overflowing and my mind is boggling; I am on overload!

The books that help you most, are those which make you think the most.

—THEODORE PARKER

Do I now do everything right? Unfortunately, I do not, as much as that is my ultimate desire. But I realize that every day is a brand-new one and I can start over again if I've really blown it in some way or another the day before.

This seems an appropriate place to insert one of my all-time-favorite quotes:

Regret for the things we did can be tempered by time; it is regret for the things we did not do that is inconsolable.

—SYDNEY J. HARRIS

That quote, written on a scrap of paper many years ago and now yellowed by age, is pasted on my bathroom mirror. The second portion of the quote—"it is regret for the things we did not do that is inconsolable"—motivated me to write my first book, *The Positive Thinker*. Lately, I've been examining the first portion, "Regret for the things we did can be tempered by time . . ."

I've come to disagree with Harris to a certain degree. Perhaps he should have said "Regret for *some* of the things," because, in examining my life, I realize that I have many regrets that can never be tempered by time. And that is another reason for this book. Over the years I am certain I have, unintentionally for the most part, made inconsiderate remarks or in other ways hurt people; definitely I have said or done things that I truly regret. Most of these indiscretions were committed out of ignorance rather than intent, but in looking back, I am horrified at my stupidity and sincerely wish I could make amends for some of my inappropriate actions that haunt me to this day.

Two of the basic tenets of most twelve-step programs seem to solve this dilemma: "Make a list of all persons we have harmed, and become willing to make amends to them all." And then, "Make direct amends to such people wherever possible, except when to do so would injure them or others."

Rationally, I know that I have undoubtedly exaggerated many of my uncomfortable memories, and that those involved would not remember if the incidents were brought to their attention after such a lapse of time. Perhaps bringing up old issues would indeed cause present-day distress. Mostly, many of the incidents involve those who are no longer living. Perhaps I am copping out. But

I've heard many wise people suggest the best thing to do to remedy guilt and other distressful feelings is to forgive yourself and then undertake to do something helpful for others here and now, in the present. And that is another reason for this book.

I sincerely hope that this small book of Commandments will prevent you from experiencing guilt and discomfort because of inadvertent, stupid, and/or inconsiderate actions. This is meant to be a guidebook for living written by one who has made many of life's mistakes and, like a fond parent, wants to shield her loved ones from doing the same.

What you will receive from this book are the pearls of wisdom I've accumulated after years of reading, digesting, and discussing countless books, in-depth conversations with others with inquiring minds, as well as my personal philosophy gleaned over, as A. E. Housman said, "my threescore years and ten."

> *The ideas I stand for are not mine.*
> *I borrowed them from Socrates.*
> *I swiped them from Chesterfield.*
> *I stole them from Jesus.*
> *And I put them in a book.*
> *If you don't like their rules, whose would you*
>   *use?*
>
> —DALE CARNEGIE

So let us examine our lives. Let us reinforce what we're doing right and improve on our weak points. Let us resolve, to the best of our abilities, to be the kind of people we really want to be.

Nothing is more exciting and rewarding than the sudden flash of insight that leaves you a changed person—not only changed, but for the better.

—ARTHUR GORDON

You will note that throughout this manuscript I rely heavily on quotations. I adore quotations and only wish that someday I may say something so profound that I will be quoted. But in the meantime, I'll stick to the masters. And here are two that bear me out:

It is a good idea for an uneducated man to read books of quotations.

—WINSTON CHURCHILL

and

A book that furnishes no quotations is, me judice, *no book—it is a plaything.*

—THOMAS LOVE PEACOCK

Now, together, let us explore the contemporary Ten Commandments for successful living. And let us enjoy and contemplate the wise words and profound knowledge of the masters sprinkled throughout this text.

Take Care of Your Body

*The body is a community made up of
its innumerable cells or inhabitants.*

—THOMAS ALVA EDISON

JUST what is your body? Is it merely, as Edison said, *"a community made up of its innumerable cells or inhabitants"*?

We know the body consists of miles of arteries, veins, blood vessels, and capillaries commanded by an exceedingly important muscle, the heart. Imagine this: Your incredible heart pumps five quarts of blood through a full circuit of your body every five minutes!

Then there are six hundred other important muscles, plus tendons and ligaments within your body, all artfully draped on the approximately 206 bones that compose your skeleton. Organs vital to the body's existence such as lungs, liver, and kidneys are carefully encased within well-designed cavities for protection.

In addition, there are many systems—the reproductive, digestive, and immune, to name a few—that keep the body functioning properly. Flesh, fat, and tissues are appropriately arranged for padding and to keep things in place. Finally, there's the skin, which, as the old song says, "keeps your insides in."

Visually, we can see the body's accoutrements: hair, nails, teeth, eyes, and ears. All vital equipment, except possibly the hair; perhaps that was put there before the advent of hats to keep the top of the scalp from sunburn. But if that's true, how does one account for baldness?

The most incredible thing about your body is that it functions twenty-four hours a day, day in and day out, whether you're awake or asleep, and it will do so for your entire life span. It keeps you breathing, your blood circulating, digests your food, and monitors your temperature and blood pressure. And that's just for starters. If you stop to think about it, and if you're like me you probably don't do that very often, the precision instrument we call our body is an incredible piece of machinery! If you could buy such a machine, can you imagine its cost?

The body was perfect when it was first designed and the original model hasn't changed an iota since the first two were placed in the Garden of Eden. Compare that accomplishment with any other mechanism you can think of. Everything else has changed and evolved over the years: cars, ships, planes, and other methods of transportation; washers, dryers, vacuum cleaners, sewing machines, and a multitude of other timesaving machines for the household; farm and construction equipment; computers and communication devices. And this doesn't begin to scratch the surface of the many other highly technical mechanisms available. You name it, all but the body have required and undergone innumerable improvements over time.

Are you a bit in awe of your body? You should be! And because your body is such an incredible, priceless machine, it behooves you to take very good care of it.

As a wise unknown said, *"If you don't take care of your body, where will you live?"*

Just what do *you* consider this magnificent thing, this body in which you live? Some call their body their *vehicle*. Although I'd heard that term for years, it was popularized in the mid-nineties by a cult called Heaven's Gate; perhaps you remember their mass suicide. Ever since, I've felt a bit uncomfortable with the term "vehicle," although it is really quite appropriate. Your body, as a vehicle, can transport you, via your two magnificent legs, to many of the places you need to go. That's just another of the body's miraculous aspects. Not only is the body the mechanism to top all others, it is self-propelling as well! Some like to refer to the body as their *house* because that is where they live. That, too, makes sense to me. Others refer to their body as their *temple*—another appropriate way to think of this remarkable mechanism.

> *Your body is the temple of the Holy Ghost which is in you, which ye have of God, and ye are not your own.*
>
> —I CORINTHIANS 6:19

Now that we've considered the body and all its wonders, let's consider *your* body and what it houses: *you.*

Nobody in the world—now or ever—is, was, or ever will be exactly like you. You are unique, incredible, and one of a kind. You are a custom-made individual, unlike any other, and can never be duplicated. They say that cloning is in our future, but I doubt it; definitely it will not come to pass while I'm on this earthly planet. Condoning cloning would be a terrible mistake. God, the Universe, Whomever or Whatever you believe in, meant for each of us to be unique individuals, with potential, talents, and abilities others do not have. That is the way it should be. Rejoice in your uniqueness, work to realize your potential, unearth your particular talents, determine your individual purpose in life, and do what you must to fulfill it.

> *Nobody can be exactly like me. Sometimes even I have trouble doing it.*
>
> —TALLULAH BANKHEAD

Because ours was a military family during The War— that's World War II—as was almost everybody's during that time, I became familiar with the term "GI." In the mid-thirties, the army used GI to refer to anything issued to its soldiers. The initials then stood for "government issue" or "general issue." The acronym was later extended to refer to anything associated with military life, as well as to the soldiers themselves; hence the term "GI Joe."

When something was issued, be it a rifle or other piece of equipment, clothing, or anything else the soldier needed, it was issued "for the duration," meaning until the end of the war. It was well understood that the recipient must take good care of what was issued because whatever it was might mean the difference between life or death. The rifle is a good example of that; take good care of your rifle and it could save your life. Misuse it and neglect to keep it clean, and it could misfire, causing injury to you, or death.

I'd like to make an analogy or two here. Let's say that instead of GI or government issue, we substitute God Issue when considering the body, and that the duration, when associated with God Issue, means for the rest of your life instead of until the end of the war, as with government issue.

The point I'm trying to make is that I like to think that our bodies are God Issue; they've been given to us by God to see us through this lifetime, and as I said before, it behooves us to take the very best care of them so that they function well and last until the end of our days.

If anything is sacred, the human body is sacred.

—WALT WHITMAN, "I Sing the Body Electric"

When you were born, you emerged as a special, unique individual, imprinted with the "you" that you would eventually become. You, as all other God Issue, came with standard equipment that has not deviated over the ages. At first glance, the only thing that might differentiate you from others is your packaging. Some God Issue comes in white packaging, others come in black, brown, yellow, or red packaging. Internally and otherwise, all feature the standard equipment; the packaging is determined by your parents and ancestors, whose genes also determine the ultimate physical you, your height and general weight, eyes and hair coloring, and all else that makes you an individual unlike any other.

Our early care, health, and imprinting were dependent on others: parents, family members, and various caregivers. But upon reaching maturity, you took over. And that's where I assume you are now, in a place where you are in charge of your life and have choice as to what you do to, with, and for your body.

Assess, accept, admire, and appreciate your body

Here is an exercise I'd like you to do. Stand in front of a full-length mirror, if you have one, wearing as little clothing as your comfort level permits; being totally undressed is even better. Look at yourself. Look at *your* self, the only you that is you. Take your time as you examine the overall, complete you from top to bottom, front and back, and from both your left and right sides.

You may like the total package as is. But if you're like most of us, you'll find lots to find fault with. Reserve judgment and concentrate on your good points. Admire your overall stature, your recognizable face and workable eyes, nose, and mouth; appreciate your ears, funny looking as they may be, and your hair, even though it may not meet your specifications, or because it's thinning, graying, or white. Check out your movable parts, flex your muscles. Note how things move and coordinate perfectly with just a minute thought from your command center, your brain. Appreciate your expanse of skin and notice how well it does its assigned job of "keeping your insides in."

Say to yourself, "I love my body." And mean it. Repeat that statement until you feel love and appreciation pulsating through every cell of your body. Then say, "I am a work of art, a gift from God." Repeat those thoughts until you grasp their full meaning.

Be grateful for the unique vehicle, home, or temple that is your body for the duration. Promise yourself that even if you've been lax in the past, henceforth you'll take the very best care of your God Issue. If you notice areas of your body that need improvement, determine to start now and continue forever to maintain your precious gift in the most appropriate manner possible.

Utilize affirmations

Affirm that you will work to become healthier and stronger. Affirm that you will achieve and maintain a weight appropriate to your individual build and muscular structure. Affirm that you will not abuse your body with substances that can harm it, like nicotine and drugs. Affirm that you will be moderate in all things, including food and drink. Affirm that you will follow basic food and nutrition rules that include drinking lots of water, eating natural foods instead of those that come from a box or are preservative-laden, and supplementing your diet with vitamins and necessary nutrients. Affirm that you will get sufficient sleep for your body's needs. Know that the outcome of your sincere affirmations will result in a more attractive, younger appearance and overall healthier body, and a happier you for as long as you live.

Affirmations are marvelous tools for achieving whatever you want in life and I like to encourage people to write their own affirmations to suit their individual needs and purposes. If you've not dealt with affirmations before, I'll give you a very brief explanation of what an affirmation is, points on how to write your own, and a few samples. For an in-depth explanation of affirmations and how to write and utilize them, refer to my book *The Positive Thinker*. Please note that the terms "affirmations," "goals," "needs," and "desires" are frequently interchangeable.

1. Affirmations must be stated in the present tense.

2. They must be stated as if the result were an actuality.

3. Goals must be definite, not vague.

These are the three most important rules. For greater effectiveness, I suggest you add the two rules that follow:

4. A feeling of gratitude, appreciation, or thankfulness must be present.

5. Experience the feeling or emotion accompanying the expected results.

Let us assume that you want to lose weight. I choose that goal because it is the most universal desire of both men and women, regardless of age. Following the above rules, you must state your goal, in the *present* tense. The present tense is "I *am*," not "I will," "I'm going to," "I expect to," "I hope to," or "I'll try."

You must state your goal as if it were an actual fact, not a wished-for or hoped-for dream. You must be definite about the result you desire, not vague.

Now let's apply these rules to your desire to lose weight. Let's say your hoped-for weight is 125 pounds. A suitable affirmation would be: "I weigh 125 pounds."

That is stated in the present tense, you are stating it as an actual fact, and 125 pounds is the definite result you wish to attain. Please note that you do not affirm in the future tense with wishful thinking added such as, "One of these days (future tense), I hope (wishful thinking) to weigh 125 pounds." You are stating your goal *as if* it were an actual fact, "I weigh 125 pounds." And in being definite about the result you wish to attain by affirming a specific figure, 125 pounds, you do not simply say, "I'd like to lose some weight." That is totally vague and thereby ineffectual.

If losing weight, or maintaining an appropriate weight is one of your goals, here are a few other weight-related affirmations to help you get started and keep you on track:

I eat sensibly and exercise regularly.

I am slim, fit, youthful, healthy, and strong.

I eat a well-balanced diet.

I enjoy fruits, vegetables, dairy products, and other nutritious foods.

I maintain an appropriate weight for my height and body build.

I enjoy feeling slim and comfortable in my clothes. (This affirmation voices your gratitude and emotion, as mentioned in rules number four and five.

Please don't feel that affirmations are reserved for losing or maintaining weight; affirmations can and should be utilized in every area of your life, including that of achieving the body you desire.

Do not abuse your body!

You've heard this message many times, but let me say it once again: "Do not abuse your body." A famous ballplayer who died a few years ago said something to this effect: "If I'd have known I'd live this long, I'd have taken better care of my body." Take heed of that message so that you don't find yourself echoing his words.

I'm not here to preach to you about things we all well know. We've all been told the hazards of smoking, excessive drinking, overeating, and drugs. But we tend to rationalize, "This little bit won't hurt. Nothing will happen to me. I'm in control." Let me just say, "Be moderate." Be careful of what you do or do not put in your body.

I recently returned from a mini–high-school reunion. I say "mini" because our big reunions are observed in years that end with 5 or 0. But because ours was a relatively small class and we have such good times together, we've been having yearly mini-reunions. At each major and mini-reunion, we're faced with the news of the illness or loss of yet another class member or two, mostly due to smoking. Almost everyone I knew took up smoking for a time during the forties and fifties; it was fashionable and the devastating health risks were not then known. Fortunately, most of us gave up the habit, if, in fact, we ever started. Presently, in my circle of friends and associates, I do not know a single smoker, and I do not have ashtrays in my home.

I can only urge you not to start or, if you presently do smoke, to do your best to stop. Do whatever it takes—nicotine patches, hypnotism, cold turkey, affirmations, positive thinking, whatever. Do not put another coffin nail—as we used to call cigarettes—in your mouth ever again. Please! The choice is yours. If for no other reason, stop smoking because, in addition to staining your teeth, it causes premature lines and wrinkles, and who needs that?

> *To cease smoking is the easiest thing I ever did.*
> *I ought to know because I've done it a thousand*
> *times.*
>
> —MARK TWAIN

Be moderate in all things!

For years I was a sun worshiper. I would lie outdoors with as little clothing as modesty permitted and bake for hours on end. I never used suntan lotion or, after it became popular, sunscreen because I wanted the sun's full force, thinking it would promote a better tan. I baked *au naturel*. Although blond and fair-skinned, I did not burn, I just tanned to a deep brown. I thought I looked good, so I indulged in my exposure to the sun year in and year out, for most of my young and middle years.

Well, I paid for that indulgence. I had one cancer removed and my overall skin is not as elastic as it probably should be, considering my age. Now, according to my doctor, there's nothing I can do to undo the damage. I still like a golden look, but I now get mine from a bottle or tube. It's too bad that a nice tan, which I always thought denoted glowing health, is bad for you. And please, stay away from tanning booths. You don't need that highly concentrated radiation. Think of the alligator with his leathery skin and turn to a self-tanner instead.

But here's some good news: Vitamin C, in topical form, may reverse visible signs of skin aging, enhance collagen production, and protect skin and the immune system from the harmful effects of the sun's rays. It's so new that the potential long-term effects have yet to be studied, but you can bet that I plan to add topical vitamin C to my next shopping list. You may want to consider it, too.

You are what you eat!

Over the years, I've probably tried every diet known to man (and especially woman). The Protein Diet, the Grapefruit Diet, the Scarsdale Diet, the Beverly Hills Diet, the Drinking Man's Diet (that one was more fun than the rest!), the Pritikin Diet; and there were many more. Most of the famous spas had their own diets that their faithful patrons swore by. And speaking of the faithful, I understand the 1957 "Pray Your Weight Away" diet book is responsible for today's multimillion-dollar Christian weight-loss industry. Now, in addition to many of the above that seem to linger on, as well as the ever-popular Weight Watchers, there are diets to suit your "food mood" and others categorized by blood type.

Food is an important part of a balanced diet.
—FRAN LEBOWITZ

If a diet existed, I usually tried it. I was never fat, just about five, ten pounds at the most, heavier than I wanted to be. That was all BE—Before Exercise. Exercise liberated me forever and ever from the necessity of dieting.

(More about the wonders of exercise and my personal exercise plan shortly.) I also utilized affirmations regularly, as mentioned a bit earlier, stating my ideal weight. I am living proof that affirmations, combined with exercise, can work! But then, my stated affirmations *included* the exercise requirement, so I was committed to following through on this physical aspect.

I'm a big lunch person. If anyone calls and wants to get together, I'm the first to say, "Let's do lunch!" Consequently, I dine out often, and when I'm with a female, upon perusing the menu, the conversation usually turns to that person's latest diet, or to diets in general.

Carolyn is one of my regular lunch people. We only go to restaurants that offer salads because, as Carolyn always says, "I only want a small salad." At our last lunch, Carolyn ordered her usual "small house salad"; I ordered an entrée salad. Before the salads arrived and while I abstained, I watched in fascination as Carolyn methodically ate her way through the entire basket of French bread, each morsel lavishly coated with sweet butter, before asking that the breadbasket be refilled, whereupon she resumed her munching. As we left the restaurant, Carolyn looked at me and said, "I don't know how you stay so slim. You ate that entire entrée salad and all I had was a tiny house salad . . ." Please, be honest with yourself. Everything that goes in your mouth—not just what you ordered—counts!

It also goes without saying that food eaten standing up in front of the stove, refrigerator, or sink also counts; morsels snatched from another's plate "just to taste" count; rich delights forced upon you by a beaming hostess who assures you that she "left all the calories in the kitchen" count; and between-meal snacks and items consumed out of boredom count. Everything that goes into your mouth, and is chewed and swallowed, counts. Be aware of what you put in your mouth!

> *Imprisoned in every fat man is a thin one wildly signaling to be let out.*
>
> —CYRIL CONNOLLY, *The Quiet Grave*

I've known Merilee for over twenty-five years. And Merilee has been trying to lose thirty obnoxious pounds since before we met. She is a very social person, but to hear her talk, life for her is on hold until she loses those thirty pounds. "As soon as I lose at least thirty pounds, I'll start traveling again . . ." "When I get rid of these thirty pounds, I'm going to start a new relationship . . ." "After I slim down, I'll resume my career and life will be fulfilling the way it used to be . . ." Obviously, Merilee is well-off financially and her career is more of a fun thing than a necessity. What is Merilee doing about the thirty-pound albatross that "weighs" her down? Other than trying every new diet that comes along, and experimenting with diet drugs, some of which have turned out to be downright dangerous and possibly life threatening, Merilee has done absolutely nothing. In other words, she has ignored exercise because, as she says, "I just don't have the time."

I have suggested to Merilee that under the circumstances, she simply love and accept herself the way she is and enjoy life. This is after my many mild suggestions about the benefits of light exercise or a walking program. Why wait for something that may not happen—the loss of thirty pounds, which by now has escalated to fifty pounds—to travel, to become involved in a relationship, or resume her career? Why not start, this minute, to love her body the way it is, and get on with her life and living? But Merilee is impatient; exercise and a walking regimen take too long. Diets and pills are bound to be quicker, she tells me and so, after twenty-five years, our dialogue continues on the same track. Amazingly, the compound in which she lives offers a workout room, tennis courts, and a golf course, as well as outdoor and indoor swimming pools. "I don't have time for that stuff," she reiterates as she munches on a chocolate from the bowl on her coffee table. "But as soon as I lose that thirty pounds, life will be wonderful again . . ."

> *Tomorrow's life is too late. Live today.*
>
> —MARTIAL, *Epigrams*

I have a friend that I bump into frequently when I walk my dog. She used to go to the same health club that I attended, so when we chat, it's usually about the battle of the bulge. She says the "Cookie Monster" does her in. Mid-to-late afternoon, she gives in to her craving and binges on cookies. "I just can't resist, then I'm mad at myself for eating the whole package. It's a real problem," she laments. I murmured something about the perils of temptation, but what I was really thinking was, "Who does the shopping at your house? Why do you allow the Cookie Monster into your kitchen cupboard at all?" Make this a rule: Don't allow food that you should not eat in the house. Why set yourself up for temptation and probable failure?

Last week, while lunching with Felicia, who was anx-

ious to rid herself of seven pesky pounds, I was told the
wonders of her latest diet. Not-allowed items included
pasta, potatoes, root vegetables such as carrots and others that grow in the ground, and all fruit "because everything turns into sugar in the body, and then the sugar
turns to fat." I expressed my skepticism, but Felicia assured me that "this is the very latest diet and everybody's on it." I suggest that it might be better to stick
to the tried-and-true food groups in moderation: fruit,
vegetables, grains, meat and other proteins, and dairy
products. She looked at me as if I'd taken leave of my
senses. "But this is the *latest* diet!" she repeated. Felicia's results are not yet in, but ask yourself, "Do I want
a healthy diet or a crash diet?"

Or a crazy diet? A woman I know well was concerned about a skin condition that would not clear up.
She is a bright, sensible, highly educated person, and set
about to do extensive personal research into what might
be causing her skin condition. Her self-diagnosis indi-
cated that it was related to the yeast family of infections,
so she undertook to eliminate anything that her medical
books suggested might contribute in any way to yeast
infections. She cut out many of the basic five food
groups and, in a very short period of time, became weak
and lethargic. One evening, she went into convulsions
and slipped into a coma, which her doctor feared might
be fatal. Thankfully, after a significant hospital stay,
long convalescence, and an appropriate, medically ap-
proved diet, she recovered and now appears to be in
good health. Why take such a chance? Let me ask again,
"Do you want a healthy diet or a crash diet?"

While we're on the subject, I have a story to tell
about myself. When I was a girl, and as a young woman,

exercise was not recognized as one of life's necessities as it is today. Somewhere along the line, when in my forties, the need for it surfaced in my life and I decided to join a health club. I knew I had to make a commitment for it to work, so I went into the club that I had chosen and, to the amazement of the woman at the desk, plunked down my membership fee for a full year without even touring the place or taking a sample class.

This began my lifelong commitment to exercise; I say it saved my life and I truly believe that. Although I looked healthy and fine, my body had been neglected and exercise was the solution. In addition to the usual classes and facilities, my club, the Best Me, offered a yearly event that they called the Blitz, a Monday-through-Friday complete diet-plus-workout, the kind you would get at an expensive spa. Naturally, I signed up.

This was many years ago, but as I remember, it basically required one's early presence at the club, three hour-long exercise sessions interspersed with talks about diet, exercise, and fashion, sessions in the steam bath and sauna, and massage. In between, we were given high-protein energy drinks for breakfast, a mid-morning snack, and lunch. After lunch, the entire group walked around Oakland's beautiful Lake Merritt, a distance of 3.9 miles. Upon our return, another protein drink was offered. When we left the club in the late afternoon, each participant took home a basket containing her low-calorie evening meal.

After the last session on Friday afternoon, there was a graduation ceremony of sorts, with a weigh-in of all participants. As each graduate stepped on the scale, her lost inches and total weight loss were announced, accompanied by much applause. One after another stepped on the scales. "Anne lost seven pounds." "Gini lost five pounds." "Karen lost ten pounds. Wow!" "Alice." Quiet. "Oops, Alice gained four pounds!" Yes, I *gained* four pounds! Evidently, I overdid it on those energy drinks; they were just so good!

That really taught me a lesson, and frankly, I immediately became sick of the whole dieting concept. I'm grateful that I no longer worry about the newest "in" diet and what I'm "allowed" to eat. I now eat what I want, and by that I mean *real* food that you chew, not popular shakes like the energy drinks that did me in; I eat when I want, and I eat what I consider to be an appropriate amount for me. Fortunately, I tend to favor salads and healthful foods, and could care less about most junk food, heavy or deep-fried items, or pastries and sweets.

But I never deprive myself. I hate deprivation in any form. Little indulgences are therapeutic, I believe, and we should never deny ourselves. Moderation is the key.

This discourse is not about dieting. It is about *not* dieting. Let me be the last one to tell you to go on a diet. I'll leave that up to you and your doctor. Because we're talking about your fabulous body, my purpose is to urge you to take the very best care of it. In that regard, eating healthful foods is vitally important. You put the appropriate gas in your car; do the same for your body. If you're not sure of the right foods to eat, there are hundreds of books available in the bookstores and at your local library that can enlighten you.

If you're from my generation, or one closely adjacent, you've probably been warned, by your parents, about the starving children in China or Europe or, more recently, in any number of Third World countries. Yes, there are starving children, and adults, in many of these places, but does your cramming and demolishing every bit of food in sight really help them? Of course not. But we all bought the concept of the Clean Plate Club and I must say that I belong to that club, to an extent, to this day.

I agree that it is a sin and a crime to waste food. I am an advocate of the waste-not, want-not group of thinkers. But I know, realistically, that it does not help the children in China or Europe or in the Third World countries if I get fat and become unhealthy on their behalf. So I endeavor to see that the food that I order in restaurants or buy for at-home consumption does not go to waste. Rather than feeling obliged to clean my plate, I ask for doggie bags or boxes when I'm out, and when at home, I package the leftovers into containers that I refrigerate for later consumption.

A neighbor whom I knew well over the years also subscribed to the Clean Plate Club, but her husband and children did not. So, not wanting to waste food or deprive the current starving children wherever in the world they were, and not liking to deal with leftovers, she took on the chore of personally cleaning all the plates after dinner, as well as finishing off what was left in the cooking pots. Slowly but surely she became fat, and then obese. She died at a relatively early age from her weight problem; her heart simply couldn't handle the overload. Even though I agree with the waste-not, want-not concept, please do not carry that, or membership in the Clean Plate Club, to extremes. Better to throw away leftovers than to become a human garbage disposal.

Since all of my above true stories were about women,

you may think that concern about the body beautiful is strictly a female thing. *Au contraire!* Many men go completely overboard in the body department, but they do it in other ways. Rather than dieting, they tend to hit the health club, their cycles, or the jogging trail.

My friend Hans, for example, has become a fitness freak. Because he was a chubby out-of-shape guy when I first met him, I introduced him to my then-current health club. He now runs marathons, cycles across continents, and when home, works out at the gym every day. This regimen certainly pays off for Hans; his weight is now ideal for his height and bone structure, he looks a good ten to fifteen years younger than his chronological age.

And my son Mark, who is gorgeous enough in face and body to be a magazine centerfold (he will kill me if he reads this!), runs up the mountain adjacent to his home every morning before going to his law office. Recently, we went to brunch to celebrate his birthday. After a moderate meal, he complained that he was uncomfortable, saying his pants and belt felt too tight, and mentioned that he had to cut back on the amount that he ate in addition to increasing his amount of exercise. Yes, men are concerned about their weight and appearance just as much as women are.

Yesterday I met Tom, an old buddy of Hans. The three of us were having lunch at one of San Francisco's most famous restaurants. To my surprise, Tom started talking about excess weight and how to lose it. Perhaps the subject was close to his heart because he has a new girlfriend who is considerably younger than he, and keeping fit and youthful is now of prime importance to him.

Tom spends much of his time in the Far East because of his work, so he maintains a home in Taiwan as well as one here in the States. He quoted a wise old Chinese woman he knows who said to him, "Taking just one small step daily will make an enormous difference over time." He went on to explain that if you want to change your diet and fruit is something you want to add, simply eating one piece of fruit each day, a banana or piece of melon for example, can get you started on a new lifelong path. By the same token, if you want to lose weight, omitting one small item daily can, over time, make a significant difference in your body. I must remember to tell my friends Carolyn, who might want to consider eliminating bread before meals, and Merilee, who desperately desires to lose thirty-plus unwanted pounds, about this simple nondiet solution. The wise Chinese woman's advice applies, obviously, to all areas of life, not only diet and food. Think about it.

And here's a simple suggestion for weight loss that I came across in a recent publication: If you're right-handed, eat with your left hand. If you're left-handed, eat with your right hand. Naturally you'll eat more slowly and therefore your "full" gauge will register before you devour everything on your plate.

If all else fails, fidget! Yes, I said "fidget" A Mayo Clinic survey conducted a few years ago to determine why some people can eat as much as they want and stay thin, while others get fatter with almost every mouthful, discovered that fidgeting burns calories. What exactly do they mean by fidgeting? One of the researchers stated, "It's something about physical activity." Another termed it "nonexercise activity thermogenesis." Although none of the researchers was precisely sure what fidgeting entailed, they stated it may have included things that most people would call fidgeting: frequently shifting position in their seats at work, crossing and uncrossing their legs, and sitting up straighter to maintain their posture. They also included behaviors that came close to what could be termed exercise: getting up to stretch, or to go to the water fountain or rest room. Keep these thoughts in mind if you have a desk job or tend to be a couch potato.

And now, hot off the press, is news that may get you off the hook if you've tried every weight-loss method available without success. A recent *Newsweek* article suggests that such problems can start in the womb. Cutting-edge research states that adult illness and problems like obesity, diabetes, cardiovascular disease, and breast cancer may have their roots before birth. "Recent research," states Dr. Peter Nathanielsz of Cornell University, in his new book, *Life in the Womb*, "provides compelling proof that the health we enjoy throughout our lives is determined to a large extent by the conditions in which we developed."

But do not immediately blame Mom for your surplus weight and other ills, and do not feel powerless because your fate may have been sealed before you were born. How you live your life here and now still matters. By virtue of your lifestyle, how you treat your body, and what you eat, you and you alone have total control over calorie and fat consumption, and other things that have an impact upon cholesterol levels, as well as many important body measurements and functions. We must continually strive to do the best we can with what we have been given.

Let's look at exercise

Whenever the urge to exercise comes upon me,
I lie down for a while and it passes.

—ROBERT MAYNARD HUTCHINS

For those of us who love to eat, albeit sensibly, exercise—more than just fidgeting—is what allows us to enjoy food without guilt. In addition to helping control weight, exercise can strengthen bones, maintain muscles and joints, and reduce risk of disease, heart attack, diabetes, high blood pressure, depression, and anxiety. It also can help to boost immunity. Yes, exercise can *add* healthful years to your life span, and best of all, as in the case of Hans, exercise has the magic ability to *subtract* years from your appearance.

And here's more good news: Exercise can reshape your body. And strength training, the use of hand weights, can sculpt muscles regardless of your age. After committing to a program of exercise and strength training, you can expect to lose a clothing size or two, and find that your overall body is becoming trimmer and firmer, more toned. Other benefits include increased vitality and strength, improved mood, and better sleep. For those who are also dieting, strength training helps prevent muscle and bone loss. You may not know it, but when you diet without exercise, much of the weight lost, in addition to water, is muscle, bone, and other lean tissue.

"Even with all the benefits considered, exercise sounds tedious," you say. "I don't have the time. I'm not into joining a gym or health club. I don't have room for a lot of expensive equipment and I don't want to

have to buy an exercise wardrobe or a bunch of videos."
Okay, I hear you. I'll tell you about my personal plan,
what I do and when I do it, and the minimal requirements for any effective exercise strength-training program. Then you decide for yourself. But I can tell you
in advance, as far as I'm concerned, a personal exercise
routine is the only way to go! I say this with all honesty,
because after decades of fighting the eternal battle of the
bulge, I believe I have found the answer—for me. I offer
it to you for your consideration. Please feel free to made
adaptations to suit your individual lifestyle and personal
schedule.

My personal plan

Basically, I do two things, and I do them, with rare exception, every day of my life. I walk for fifty minutes daily,
and I exercise at home for twenty minutes each and every
day, alternating floor exercises with strength-training exercises utilizing hand weights. The walk addresses my
aerobic needs, and the floor and strength-training exercises
take care of my body- and muscle-toning requirements.
This combination works well for me, and has for a good
long time. Before you throw your hands up in despair—
screaming, "Impossible! I don't have that kind of time or
energy"—remember, I'm merely passing along my personal routine *for your consideration only*. Please feel free
to make whatever adaptations you feel necessary to accom-
modate your schedule.

First, the walk. As I said, I walk for fifty minutes
daily. Why fifty minutes rather than thirty minutes or
one hour? Simply because that's the amount of time it

takes me to cover my route. I live in a hilly area, so my route was determined long ago by the least amount of uphill combined with the most amount of level territory. If you don't have fifty minutes or even thirty, walk for twenty minutes—or just ten minutes—but *walk*. Walk off the weight during your lunch hour if there is no other time in your busy schedule. But do it—please! Walk daily if you can. If you can't walk daily, walk as often and *regularly* as you can—regularity is the key. In addition to looking better over time, you'll feel better *instantly*. Not only is it the easiest exercise routine going, but walking is the most popular workout worldwide; over seventy-six million people do it. If you're average, you'll walk a total of 100,000 miles in your lifetime.

I walk with my dog, Charlie, and although he wishfully harbors thoughts of pit stops and tree and telephone-pole sniffing, he knows that moving along at a brisk pace is his obligation. Unless there's something unusual on my agenda, such as an early-evening meeting or special event, we always walk just before dinner. Charlie knows at the end of the walk he'll receive his reward, his evening meal, and I allow myself a reward, too—a glass of wine. I'm big on rewards, and you might like to look into them for yourself as well.

Walking is easy and doesn't require anything other than a good, sturdy, comfortable pair of walking shoes. When I say walking shoes, I mean the athletic type of shoe made by such companies as Reebok, Adidas, and many others, rather than what you might consider a comfortable pair of dress shoes or loafers from your regular wardrobe. Simply put on your walking shoes, and clothing appropriate to the weather and temperature, and step out of your door and into the outside world. Walking three times a week should be the bare minimum; more is better, of course. Start slowly, say twenty minutes at a time, and increase both the length of your walk and the number of days.

I walk year-round regardless of the weather; the only time I don't is during thunder and lightning storms. Where I live in California, that might occur once every five years! We do have a lot of rain, though, in fact we have a three-month-minimum rainy season every year and that can pose a problem, more so for Charlie than for me. His coat is very thick and dense and his fur is long; when he comes in soaking wet, the room in which he shakes off gets a thorough sprinkling. I recently found a raincoat for him that seems as though it might help that situation; he'll wear it at the first sign of this year's showers.

My rain gear is a waterproof jacket and shower cap, and with a chapeau like that, I am probably the laughingstock of Crocker Highlands! This ridiculous look came after much trial and error. Umbrellas simply don't work with Charlie in tow, as his exuberance frequently requires both hands on the leash and my jacket's hood hampers my peripheral vision. So I wear a shower cap, the type given away at hotels, and the heck with what observers might think! And there *are* observers. I'm constantly running into people away from my walking route, whom I've never seen before, who stop me on the street or in stores to ask me if I'm the lady with the little white dog who walks down their street daily. It's a strange feeling to realize you're being observed when you least expect it. So far, no one has mentioned my shower cap!

After the walk and a sip of wine, I launch into my

exercise routine. By this time, it's close to seven P.M., probably the most inappropriate time in the world to start one's exercise routine, and I don't advocate it for you; I'm simply telling you what I do and I suggest you adapt your routine to your personal time clock. Recently, I read the following: "Morning exercisers stick with it longer than afternoon or evening exercisers. After a year, 75 percent still exercise versus 50 percent of midday and only 25 percent of evening people."

I am not a morning person and am becoming less of one as each year passes. Since I must sleep late because of my frequent bouts of middle-of-the-night insomnia, I don't do much of anything in the morning except read the daily paper. Then I have an early lunch (as you know, I'm a lunch person!) and in the afternoon, I write.

You must figure out what's best for you and then stick to it. The last three words, *stick to it,* are the important part, and my book *Putting the Positive Thinker to Work: 21 Ways and 21 Days to a Happy, Fulfilling, Successful Life* explains the twenty-one-day, or three-week commitment process that I felt was important enough to devote an entire book to. I mention this not as a plug, but to emphasize the importance of doing something daily until it becomes a habit. It is a scientific fact that it takes the human body twenty-one days to adjust to new behavior, after which it will become habit, and then, supposedly, you're home free! Your new behavior is incorporated into your routine, and if you renege, you get a bad case of the guilts—or at least I do.

I worked out for years at health clubs and gyms; in fact, I used to brag that I exercised for fifteen years without missing a day. In retrospect, I was probably exaggerating, but it was close; I do believe I allowed myself to take Sundays off. Then I broke my leg by doing crazy high-impact aerobics; that was followed by a back injury because I continued to exercise while in the leg cast. This ended gyms for me; I decided to exercise at home and I've been doing so for over ten years. This works far better for me, especially time- and convenience-wise, and it fits nicely into my personal schedule.

As mentioned earlier, I alternate my two exercise routines: floor exercises for abdominals and inner thighs, and strength-training exercises utilizing free weights for arms and upper body. I figure my legs get a major workout daily with my fifty-minute Charlie walks, so the only other legwork I do is for inner thighs. These exercises, which I do in my bedroom while the TV plays in the background, can be utilized by both men and women. I prefer this type of exercise routine to those on video made popular by some models, movie stars, and exercise gurus. I find the latter, which are usually highly aerobic, require more room than I have available, and their pace is often faster or more frenetic than mine. My aerobic requirements are met by my walk; my strength-training and toning requirements are met by my indoor exercise routine.

The following is a combination of exercises remembered from past health clubs and exercise studios, those pictured in magazines, and a specialized routine devised for me by a personal trainer, a birthday gift from a friend. Over the years, I've added new exercises and discarded others because I became bored with them, or simply didn't like them anymore. So my exercises have evolved into an eclectic routine, but one that works for me and could for you as well.

Routine 1—Floor Exercises

Exercise One: Basic Crunches

POSITION: Lie on the floor on your back with knees bent and feet flat. Place right hand behind your head with elbow out to the side. Place left hand on your midsection. This is so that you can feel your muscles in action. Tilt your pelvis toward your upper body so that your abs, or abdominals, press into the floor. (See figure 1.)

ACTION: Slowly curl your torso upward until head and shoulders lift from the floor, then lower.

I do fifty reps, or repetitions.

Figure 1

VARIATION 1: Reverse hands. Place left hand behind your head with elbow out to the side. Place right hand on your midsection. Continue as above. This exercise tightens and tones your entire midsection. (See figure 2.)

I do fifty reps.

Figure 2

VARIATION 2: Place both hands behind head. With knees together, turn both knees to right. Lift and curl to the left. (See figure 3.)

Figure 3

VARIATION 3: Same as above, except turn both legs to the left. Lift and curl to the right. Variation 2 and 3 are for the obliques, the side muscles that help define your waist. (See figure 4.)

I do fifty reps each of #2 and #3

Figure 4

VARIATION 4: Place both hands behind head, elbows out to sides. Curl up for three counts, release down for one count. This is another exercise for the midsection. I do thirty-five reps. Why thirty-five instead of fifty? This one is a bit more strenuous, and besides, I don't like it!

Exercise Two: Abdominal Killer

POSITION: Lie on the floor with knees bent and feet flat, hands behind head with elbows out. (See figure 5.)

ACTION: Bring elbows and upper body to knees and knees to chest; as you lower upper body, extend legs out straight as close to the floor as possible. (See figure 6.) As the name implies, this abdominal exercise can be a killer at first, so go slowly and build up reps.

I do thirty-five reps.

Figure 5   Figure 6

Exercise Three: Modified Crunch

POSITION: Lie on the floor with hands behind head, elbows out. Legs are extended upward with knees slightly flexed. (See figure 7.)

ACTION: Lift and lower upper body. This is also an abdominal exercise.

I do thirty-five reps.

Figure 7

Exercise Four: The "W"

POSITION: Lie on floor with hands behind slightly raised head or under hips, to support lower back. Legs are raised with knees bent and feet off the floor. (See figure 8.)

ACTION: With legs together, thrust them straight up in the air; bring them down to starting position, and with next thrust, extend them out to sides. (See figure 9.) I visualize this as a "W" movement. This is for inner thighs.

I do thirty-five reps.

Figure 8   *Figure 9*

Exercise Five: Diagonal Leg Lift

POSITION: Lie stretched out on left side on floor, left elbow bent with head resting on bent arm. (See figure 10.)

ACTION: Lift right leg straight up with slight diagonal backward movement. You will feel a tightening in buttocks (See figure 11.) This is a "bun" exercise. Do the same thing on other side.

I do thirty-five reps of each.

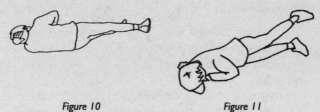

Figure 10   Figure 11

Exercise Six: Leg Lift

POSITION: Lying on back with knees bent, feet flat on floor. Turn right leg out to the side with knee slightly bent. (See figure 12.)

ACTION: Lift and lower leg. Repeat the action with the left leg.

I do thirty-five reps.

Figure 12

Exercise Seven: Leg Kick

POSITION: Lying on back with knees bent, feet flat on floor. Turn right leg out to the side with knee slightly bent. (See figure 13.)

ACTION: Kick right leg out to a straight position and back. Repeat the same action with the left leg. Exercise seven is for inner thighs.

I do thirty-five reps of each.

Figure 13

Exercise Eight: The Modified Push-up

POSITION: Face the floor with hands outstretched at shoulder level; weight of body is on the knees. (See figure 14.)

ACTION: Lower body to floor and lift. This exercise is for upper arms. I include it in this series of floor exercises because it seems to fit. (See figure 15.)

I do fifty reps.

Figure 14   Figure 15

For years, I did the above routine on my carpeted floor. Between Charlie's shedding hair, which cannot be controlled, and inadequate carpet padding, this finally became unsatisfactory. I was forced to search the garage (which resulted in a much-needed cleaning) for my old exercise mat. The mat has made a great difference in the ease and comfort of this routine. Mats are readily available at sporting-goods and fitness-equipment stores at a very nominal cost. I slide my mat under the bed when not in use.

Routine 2—Strength Training with Free Weights

After doing Exercise One, Variations 1 through 4 below, on the floor for some time, I purchased a plastic step stool (available at sporting-goods and fitness-equipment stores) in order to give my arms a better workout. I put a bath towel over the step stool, as I don't like the feel of cold plastic next to my back. The step stool allows me to begin the exercise action slightly below shoulder level, since the shoulders are elevated by the stool. This is an individual preference; please do not feel that a step stool is necessary for these exercises.

I suggest you buy pairs of dumbbells in five-, eight-,

and ten-pound weights. You'll also need a sturdy chair (in my case, I use the love seat on which Charlie sleeps). I wear comfortable clothes that don't restrict and my athletic shoes. If you are a total novice, you may want to start with three-pound weights, but you'll rapidly progress to the heavier ones when your body becomes accustomed to the training.

Take it slowly and do not overdo. After one of my first sessions, in which I obviously did too much, I was alarmed to note that my arm muscles were so shaky that I could barely sign my name for hours!

I started with five-pound weights, and was soon using eights. I have now progressed to tens, but when doing Exercise Two, Dumbbell Flyes, I feel a definite back strain, so with that exercise, I plan to stay with eights for the time being.

Exercise One: Overhead Press

POSITION: Lie with back on step stool if you have one; otherwise, lie on floor with legs bent, feet flat on floor. Hold a dumbbell, or weight, in each hand, elbows bent. (See figure 16.)

ACTION: Extend arms straight up, then lower. (See figure 17.)

I do three sets of twelve reps.

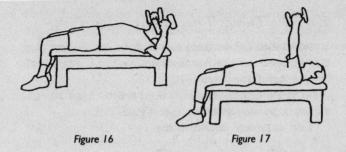

Figure 16   Figure 17

Exercise Two: Dumbbell Flye

POSITION: Lie on step stool or floor, knees bent, feet flat on floor. Arms are extended overhead with palms facing, a dumbbell in each hand. (See figure 18.)

ACTION: Extend arms out to sides as far as comfortable, return to starting position. (See figure 19.)

I do three sets of twelve reps.

Figure 18   Figure 19

Exercise Three: Triceps Extension Press

POSITION: Lie on step stool or floor, knees bent, feet flat on floor. Arms are straight up overhead, a dumbbell in each hand. (See figure 20.)

ACTION: Lower arms backward behind head by ears, return to starting position. (See figure 21.)

I do three sets of twelve reps.

Figure 20   Figure 21

Exercise Four: Seated Lateral Shoulder Flye

POSITION: Sit on chair (I sit on my love seat). Bend over with arms straight, hands near feet. (See figure 22.)

ACTION: Lift arms straight out to shoulder level, return to starting position. (See figure 23.)

I do two sets of twelve reps.

Figure 22

Figure 23

Exercise Five: Biceps Curl

POSITION: Stand with feet apart, knees slightly flexed. Hold a dumbbell in each hand at hip level. (See figure 24.)

ACTION: Lift to waist, lower. (See figure 25.)

VARIATION 1: Position same as above, except hands are at waist level. Raise to shoulders and lower.

VARIATION 2: Position same as above, hands at hip level. Lift all the way to shoulders and lower.

I do two sets of six reps of each of the above.

Figure 24

Figure 25

Exercise Six: Biceps Curl with Twist

POSITION: Stand with feet apart, knees slightly flexed. Hold a dumbbell in each hand (figure 26) (knuckles are up).

ACTION: Flex up as in previous biceps curl (clenched fingers up), but twist hands toward each other as they reach chest level. Lower and repeat.

I do two sets of twelve reps.

Figure 26

Figure 27

Exercise Seven: Triceps Kickback

POSITION: Stand with feet apart, lean forward with knees slightly bent. (See figure 28.)

ACTION: Reach and extend arms backward. Return to starting position. (See figure 29.)

I do two sets of twelve reps.

Figure 28

Figure 29

Exercise Eight: One-Arm Row

POSITION: Place left knee on chair or love seat, right foot on floor. Dumbbell is held in right hand. (See figure 30.)

ACTION: Raise right arm backward, then forward in a sawing motion. Repeat the action with your left arm.

I do two sets of twelve reps.

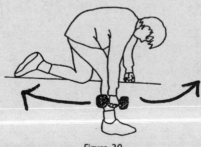

Figure 30

Exercise Nine: Standing Lateral Plus for Shoulders

POSITION: Standing with feet apart, arms at sides, a dumbbell in each hand.

ACTION: Raise arms to the side and up to shoulder level, palms facing down. (See figure 31.) While at shoulder level, swing arms to center in front of body (figure 32), lower to front of thighs. (See figure 33.) Then reverse, raising arms to shoulder level in front of body (figure 34), swing out to shoulder level (figure 35) at sides, lower (figure 36). Repeat entire series.

I do one set of twelve reps.

Figure 31

Figure 32

Figure 33

Figure 34

Figure 35   Figure 36

Exercise Ten: Front Raises

POSITION: Standing with a dumbbell in each hand, arms in front of thighs.

ACTION: Raise straight arms to shoulder level, alternately, in front of body. Lower to starting position, repeat. (See figure 37.)

I do two sets of twelve reps.

Figure 37

The general idea with weights is to start with light weights and more frequent reps and, when you no longer feel challenged, increase to heavier weights and less frequent reps, increasing the number of reps gradually. So, over time, you increase both weight and reps. Never attempt to lift weights that seem too heavy. Pain is not appropriate, regardless of the old saying, "No pain, no gain." Pain is a signal that you are going beyond your personal limits.

I have mentioned that I walk and exercise daily. I don't advocate my strict daily schedule for any but the compulsive or totally dedicated, both of which I tend to be.

> *Nothing to excess.*
>
> —SOLON

On the other hand—

> *Nothing succeeds like excess.*
>
> —OSCAR WILDE

As previously stated, I suggest you walk three days per week minimum, with five being far better. As far as the two exercise routines, decide first how often you can or are willing to commit and then *commit*. You can alternate your routine so that you do floor exercises one day and strength exercises the next.

> *The body says what words cannot.*
>
> —MARTHA GRAHAM

Let's talk about image!

Now that you're on the way to a perfect body, how do you plan to package it for the world to see? This is the time to reinvent yourself and become the person you've always dreamed of being.

> *It's never too late to be what you might have been.*
>
> —GEORGE ELIOT (pseudonym for Mary Ann Evans)

Maybe you've always felt plain and ordinary. But why continue? You're changing your body; it's becoming healthier, stronger, better looking, and more appealing. Let's change your image to suit the new you.

Just what is image? Webster offers many definitions; the one that seems to apply most aptly in this instance is "impression." Perhaps the word "look" might also apply. How do you want to be perceived? What kind of impression do you *now* make? What kind of impression do you *want* to make?

Some well-known names come to my mind when thinking of image: Audrey Hepburn, Jackie Kennedy Onassis, and Princess Di connote elegance and sophistication; Katharine Hepburn makes me think of independence; Mother Teresa of suffering, love, and compassion. Many actors and musicians, both male and female, have developed personal looks or images. Gerry Spence, the attorney from Wyoming, would not have the same impact in the courtroom without his western boots and hat; TV's detective Columbo has certainly become memorable because of his vintage raincoat and perennial cigar.

In thinking of those in my personal circle of friends, I realize that the majority of them have unique personal looks, or images, which developed over time simply because of who they are and their individual lifestyles. This uniqueness is carried over into their homes and decor, which run the gamut from earthy to elegant, eclectic to eccentric. Their choice of cars is usually predictable, as is the clothes and jewelry they wear. Everything, it seems, makes a statement.

Speaking of making a statement, one of the easiest ways to do so is to wear a hat. Patricia Fripp, one of the very best professional speakers on the circuit worldwide, always wears a hat. I've never seen her without one. She is the personification of the word "petite"; I expect she started wearing hats in order to be noticed when she first began speaking. She now has so many hats that, for charity, she once offered a showing of her personal hat wardrobe to the public. I'm certain she raised a considerable sum.

My friends Connie and Florenzi both wear hats frequently and they always look smashing. San Francisco's flamboyant mayor, Willie Brown, is known for his fedoras and other headgear. And his extensive hat wardrobe has made his hat seller, Ruth Dewson, famous.

> *Yankee Doodle came to town*
> *Riding on a pony*
> *He stuck a feather in his hat*
> *And called it macaroni.*

> —Anonymous, used in the ballad opera
> *The Disappointment* by ANDREW BARTON

Doesn't that bring a mental picture to mind? And while you're thinking of hats, can you imagine your favorite country-western singer without his or her Stetson? Davy Crockett without his coonskin cap? Hitchcock without his homburg? Fred Astaire without his top hat? Or Monica without her beret?

My friend Allen gave a Mad Hatter party for his sixtieth birthday; everyone attending was encouraged to wear a hat. I rummaged around in my closet and found one that I bought years ago but never wore. At one time, hats were my passion; I think it came as a result of a bad haircut, so I happen to have a few lurking in the dark confines of my closet. I then had to find something appropriate to go with the chosen hat. I pulled out a long slinky teal dress with jacket that matched the ribbon on the hat perfectly.

The party was held at San Francisco's Ritz-Carlton hotel. In trying to locate the correct ballroom, I rode an elevator or two and traversed a couple of hallways.

A man in one of the elevators said, "You are the most elegant lady I've seen in years!" In the hallway, I received a second compliment that began with "Wow!" It was almost equal to the first. Can you imagine how exhilarated I felt? And it was all due to my wearing a hat!

Hats can definitely create a look. But so can jewelry. Barbara creates the most fabulous neckpieces I've ever seen anywhere. Her clients include well-known names in show business, politics, and society. Her pieces are so expensive that just one can equal the cost of a small car. Those fortunate enough to own one usually wear theirs frequently, thereby making it their signature piece to create the image or look they want; the wealthy collect Barbara's pieces as status symbols. I'm not saying you have to spend a small fortune in order to find a signature piece; perhaps a piece of family jewelry that you could wear regularly might fit the bill.

Forgetting hats and jewelry, which are just accoutrements after all, what is *your* basic, overall look? In thinking of some of my friends, Marilyn's look is expensive, Florenzi is eclectic, Barbara is elegantly exotic, Fern is artistically basic. And Alice? I can't peg myself, but outside of occasional instances like my Ritz-Carlton experience (yes, I can put on the dog when necessary) I expect you could call me a Gap gal. I feel most comfortable in T-shirts and shorts or khakis in moderate weather, and sweats when it's cooler. When I was in radio and TV, I think I could have been called "executive," but that was when I had to wear attire appropriate for my office and daily appearances on TV. Now no one sees me in my upstairs writing office at home, so I have no need to impress anyone or project an image. I expect that, in itself, *is* projecting an image!

Now it is up to you to decide upon a new image, if indeed a new one is appropriate. Of course it goes without saying that you'll always be bandbox clean, pressed, and polished regardless of what you're doing, with freshly shampooed hair and well-groomed nails. And regardless of the image you've decided to portray, *always* believe you're beautiful. As Sophia Loren said, "Nothing makes a woman more beautiful than the *belief* that she is beautiful."

> *People should be beautiful in every way—in their faces, in the way they dress, in their thoughts and in their innermost selves.*
>
> —ANTON CHEKHOV

Chekhov's quote reminds me to mention that when discussing image, we're not just talking about the *physical* you, but the *entire* you, including your thoughts and innermost self. If you are, as my friend Bonnie said of herself last week over lunch, "insecure and full of low self-esteem," now is the time to change all that. I never knew that Bonnie felt that way; she always seemed totally confident, so I was amazed at her confession and self-deprecation.

> *Nobody holds a good opinion of a man who has a low opinion of himself.*
>
> —ANTHONY TROLLOPE, *Orley Farm*

For this problem, Doctor Alice prescribes the following affirmations from *The Positive Thinker*. I suggest you repeat them until you truly believe them:

I am the best that I can be. I do whatever is necessary to improve myself.

I always maintain a positive mental attitude.

Every day in every way I am getting better and better.

I am confident, self-assured, and optimistic.

I am worthy to receive all that I ask.

I deserve to be happy, healthy, prosperous, and successful.

Sleep, is it a waste of time?

Deprive me of anything but sleep.

—ALICE POTTER

In talking about the body and its care, there is one thing we cannot omit in our discussion, and that is sleep. No matter who we are or where we are on life's continuum, a good night's sleep is of utmost importance. I know this as well or better than 99 percent of the population because I fight the battle daily, or, I should say, nightly. I am one of those whose mind races madly at three A.M., or thereabouts, with great ideas for new books, chapter revisions of the present one, as well as writing enticing drafts of speeches I plan to deliver, and I simply cannot turn my galloping mind off. It's a good thing that I don't write novels or mystery stories; unusual plot twists and the need for the ultimate surprise ending would certainly contribute to an even greater state of total wide-awakeness! Then I start worrying about my next day's schedule and how I will possibly be able to cope, and the resultant anxiety once and for all chases the ever-elusive sandman from my bedroom. From what I read in newspapers and magazines, I have plenty of bleary-eyed company.

> *The beginning of health is sleep.*
>
> —IRISH PROVERB

I am fortunate that my schedule allows me great flexibility. Even though I toss the night away, by dawn I am so totally exhausted that I finally do fall into an REM sleep—that's the kind with dramatic dreams; evidently my brain is sorting out the scripts and plots I've played with during those grueling hours—and that sleep lasts until about ten A.M. Naturally this kills most of the morning, but it works for me. Every telephone message

I've left in the past five years has said, "Call me anytime *after* ten A.M.!" Unfortunately, those who don't understand assume that I am being totally indulgent, that getting by on four to six hours of sleep, maximum, a night is somehow more honorable.

Skimping on sleep is not honorable, it is unhealthy, and it will catch up with you in many ways sooner or later. Studies prove that sleep deprivation can make you sick, fat, and prematurely old. Lack of sleep plays havoc with important hormones, it harms brain cells and depletes the immune system, and it promotes the growth of fat instead of muscle. Not only that, new studies show that sleep deprivation may even accelerate the aging process! Who needs or wants any of that? Your body has done its daily job of performing every function perfectly; please give your body the rest it deserves.

> *Life is something to do when you can't get to sleep.*
>
> —FRAN LEBOWITZ

I do not have an answer to the dilemma of middle-of-the-night sleeplessness, and because I'm not a doctor, I'll not attempt to give you medical solutions or suggestions. All I can do is tell you what I do to make those anxious hours more tolerable. I suggest you give the following a try.

If you're concerned that you'll forget something important that you must remember to do the next day:

1. Recite your ABC's. This is from *The Positive Thinker*, page 26. In brief: Assign a word that you

can easily picture to every letter of the alphabet; actually A through E should be sufficient for starters. For example, A = Apple, B = Ball, C = Cat, D = Dog, E = Elephant. Then associate your middle-of-the-night worries with each letter, starting with A. Let's say you're worried that you may forget to make your tax payment and get in trouble with the IRS; associate A, or Apple, with the IRS. Picture an apple wrapped in your tax return. Next concern: You must pick up your important prescription at the drugstore tomorrow; B is for Ball, so you picture yourself throwing a ball at the front of the drugstore. Continue through the alphabet until you run out of worries and concerns. In the morning, simply recite your ABC's and retrieve the worrisome thoughts that were keeping you awake.

2. Speak your worrisome thoughts/concerns into a tape recorder. If you have a portable tape recorder, place it beside your bed, and without turning on the light, speak into it and let it all out; get it off your chest. Then forget everything until morning.

3. Write in the dark (putting on the light will only exacerbate the problem). Note your worries on a pad beside your bed. Your penmanship may leave much to be desired, but you'll probably be able to decipher the message in the A.M. Once your thoughts are written down, your mind will clear and allow you to go to sleep.

For general anxiety:

1. Count your blessings. You can't overdo this one. All too often we become so concerned with the prob-

lems of our daily existence that we forget how fortunate we are. When I become overwhelmed, especially in the middle of the night, I say, "Wait a minute, Alice. Please remember how blessed you are." That's all I need to do. I then recite my blessings, and I do it over and over, if necessary. As a rule, this allows me to relax enough to go to sleep, or, if not, to lie in bed peacefully without tossing and turning.

Saying Peace, peace; when there is no peace.
—JEREMIAH 6:14 and 8:11

2. Pray. This is a part of the Count Your Blessing method. When I give thanks for my blessings, I am talking to my Heavenly Father. You may want to have a personal conversation with a Higher Power or the One you feel closest to. Just say, "I need Your help," and know that it will come.

3. Cast the burden. In one of my favorite books, *The Game of Life and How to Play It,* Florence Scovel Shinn talks about "Casting the Burden." Briefly, this means that we are not meant to bear the burden (worries, concerns, etc.) but that we should cast the burden upon the Lord, or the subconscious mind within, and go free. Shinn says that "Man violates law if he carries a burden, and a burden is an adverse thought or condition, and this thought or condition has its root in the subconscious." It took me a while to "get" this, but now I find it very helpful. Perhaps it will help you to find peace and, therefore, sleep.

And now, as I close this chapter, let me say to you what I always said at the end of my late-night radio broadcast, *Alice in Slumberland:*

> *Night night, sleep tight. And remember, I love you!*

>   **—ALICE POTTER**

And I *do* love you!

My Resolutions

In regard to Commandment I, *Take Care of Your Body,* these are my resolutions:

....
....
....
....
....
....
....
....
....
....
....
....
....
....
....
....
....
....
....
....
....
....
....
....
....

Expand Your Mind

All that is comes from the mind; it is based on the mind, it is fashioned by the mind.

—THE PALI CANON

AND just what exactly *is* the mind? *Webster* defines mind as "the element or complex of elements in an individual that feels, perceives, thinks, wills, and especially reasons." Does "complex of elements" mean that the power of the mind rests in such things as nerve cells, dendrites, synapses, and neurotransmitters? How does the brain enter into this definition? Is there a distinction between the mind and the brain?

In a newspaper article reporting a recent meeting in Los Angeles of the Society for Neuroscience, a renowned brain expert noted that the brain has one trillion nerve cells, each with ten thousand connections. It was also noted that "the central nervous system is a dense jungle of interconnected structures, circuits and neurotransmitter soups." There was no mention of the mind in the article. Whether mind, brain, or both, I'm impressed with the equipment that I carry around at the top of my spinal column and between my ears. I hope you are proud of yours as well.

Considerable attention has been paid to the mind/ brain controversy over the years and it's bound to continue as new discoveries are made. In *Your Maximum Mind,* Herbert Benson, M.D., quotes the famous Canadian neurosurgeon Wildre Penfield, who wrote in *The Mystery of the Mind* that the workings of the mind will probably always be impossible to explain simply on the basis of electrical or chemical action in the brain and nervous systems. "The mind is independent of the brain," he declared. "The brain is a computer, but it is programmed by something outside of itself, the mind." In regard to defining the "mind," Benson says, "In scientific terms, we simply can't be definitive. The mind certainly resides in large part in the brain; in many ways, it also seems to go beyond individual brain components."

What we call a mind is nothing but a heap or collection of different perceptions, united together by certain relations and supposed, though falsely, to be endowed with a perfect simplicity and identity.

—DAVID HUME

I agree with Benson, the mind is too awesome to define. So let's stop being so technical and get to the basic business of Commandment II, *Expand Your Mind,* for, as the advertising slogan for the United Negro College Fund states, "A mind is a terrible thing to waste." Because a closed or "unexpanded" mind is a wasted mind, let's start now to explore the many ways we can expand our minds and enrich our lives at the same time.

Read any good books lately?

To me, the fastest, easiest, simplest, and most pleasurable way to expand the mind is to read. I am in total agreement with Thomas Jefferson, who said, *"I cannot live without books."* This caused me many problems as a young girl. For some unknown reason, my mother was neither pleased nor impressed with my love of books and the fact that my nose seemed always to be stuck in one. She often suggested that I should be doing "other things." Actually, she probably wished I'd volunteer to do household chores, or to help in the kitchen. To Mother, almost anything was preferable to reading, which she took to be a form of complete and total lazy indulgence.

On the other hand, everything in print that came into our household was censored prior to being deemed fit for my consumption. The daily paper, as well as *Life, Look, The Saturday Evening Post, Collier's,* and other magazines of that day often had gaps where pictures, paragraphs, and occasionally entire articles had been removed. Even though I frequently questioned this, I was never told the real reason: Mother did not want me exposed to things she felt were beyond my years and, definitely, anything that had any relationship whatsoever to sex.

An interesting sideline to this is that when Mother felt she could no longer cope, I was bundled off to my grandmother's for a few days, occasionally longer. Grandma was a warm, wonderful, down-to-earth, fun-filled lady with a zest for life and a spirited sense of humor who could tell a joke with the best of them. Some of my fondest memories as a youngster are of sitting around the kitchen table with Grandma and her cronies listening to story after story and enjoying the hearty laughter that filled the air.

On the other hand, Grandma could astound you with her elegance. Often the two of us, Grandma, newly marcelled and dripping diamonds and furs, accompanied by three-or-four-year-old Alice, would sweep into a fashion show, fancy tearoom, exclusive shop, or some highfalutin social affair with the kind of chutzpah one normally associates with celebrities of the highest level.

Grandma loved Walter Winchell and radio soap operas, but her passion was detective magazines. Those magazines, which seem to have disappeared from today's newsstands, were really trashy and I haven't seen anything like them for many years; perhaps the tabloids took their place. But in those long-ago days, detective magazines were popular, and Grandma had every issue of every one ever published. And they were all over her house; how Mother missed them is beyond me, because Grandma never attempted to hide them. I'm certain that Grandma was totally unaware of the censorship that existed in her daughter's home.

Grandma put no restrictions on my reading. At her house, I could loll in bed all day reading the books that I had checked out from the library, along with her detective magazines. It didn't take me long to realize that a dictionary was in order when reading about serial killers, ax murderers, as well as a variety of sex crimes and other perversions graphically explained in her magazines, so I smuggled a dictionary from home and did I ever get an education! I am certain that unknown to Mother, I gained a greater knowledge of the seamy side of life through the magazines and my trusty dictionary than she could possibly have acquired in her entire eighty-plus years of life.

A little learning is a dangerous thing.

—ALEXANDER POPE

In those early days, my favorite books were heartrending animal stories, but only if they had a happy ending, of course. As a preteen, I graduated to the Nancy Drew books and others of that type and era. In retrospect, maybe that sort of reading was an indulgence, because it did little to expand my mind, but at least it fostered a love of books that has not only lasted to this day but, over the years, has grown by leaps and bounds. Definitely, becoming an early reader and avid book lover increased my reading skills and expanded my vocabulary, in addition to giving me a glimpse of life outside of my own little world.

We shouldn't teach great books, we should teach a love of reading.

—B. F. SKINNER

I was a frequent visitor to our local library, and on every visit, I'd leave with a load of books in my arms. Then I was faced with the problem of being allowed to read them without argument. My favorite time and place for reading was in bed at night just before going to sleep, and on weekend mornings upon awakening. This was verboten all the way around. "Beds are made for sleeping, not reading," Mother would state firmly, in her most authoritative voice. So the library books and flashlights smuggled under the covers were confiscated and hidden; the books, perhaps, to be perused for appropriateness prior to their release for Alice's reading. Then Mother couldn't remember where she stashed the books and the library fines started mounting. Even at two cents a day, which is what fines were at that time, a quarter-a-week allowance did not go far. I expect there are still some books among the missing from those days of yore!

Perhaps it was also the fact that Mother worried that reading in bed, especially with a flashlight, would somehow destroy my eyes, because I was occasionally allowed to read material she deemed appropriate while sitting on a straight dining-room chair (this to encourage proper posture) strategically placed in front of a window with sufficient light coming over the correct shoulder. Since becoming an adult, I take great pleasure in reading in bed at night, and my morning does not get off to a proper start unless I read the daily paper, in bed, before rising to dress and prepare for the day's challenges. Somehow, childishly I suppose, this gives me a sort of perverse satisfaction! I shall never, ever again read sitting in a straight dining-room chair with sufficient light coming over the correct shoulder!

> *Only one hour in the normal day is more pleasurable than the hour spent in bed with a book before going to sleep, and that is the hour spent in bed with a book after being called in the morning.*
>
> —ROSE MACAULAY

I am not suggesting that *you* read in bed, only that you *read*. In *The Tatler,* it is said that "Reading is to the mind what exercise is to the body." If you want to expand your mind, you must exercise it, and reading is one of the best mind exercises going. "What to read?" you may ask. The choice is practically endless, as a visit to your local library or any major bookstore will attest.

Recently, I saw a much-touted list of the hundred best English-language novels of the twentieth century and I anxiously perused it to see how many I had read. Not enough, I must admit. So I was heartened to hear from many sources that the list was actually a sort of promotional gimmick from the editorial board of the Modern Library, which compiled it. Nevertheless, those on the list are considered "classics." Of that term Mark Twain said, "Classic: A book which people praise and don't read."

Some of the famous names on the list of one hundred are James Joyce, F. Scott Fitzgerald, Aldous Huxley, William Faulkner, D. H. Lawrence, Joseph Heller, and John Steinbeck. Although I am not as avid a reader of novels as I am of other kinds of books, you certainly cannot go wrong by reading anything authored by the distinguished group represented by the Modern Library.

A couple of years ago, I came across an article written by K. L. Billingsley about the late Louis L'Amour, who was not included in the aforementioned list but probably should have been if for no other reason than the fact that there are one hundred million copies of his books in print.

L'Amour had a philosophy about learning and education: "Everyone is self-educated." He felt strongly that there was a difference between education and schooling. "No one can ˜get' an education," L'Amour wrote, "for of necessity education is a continuing process. No matter how much I admire our schools, I know that no university can provide an education." What a university can give is "an outline, to give the learner a direction and guidance. The rest one has to do for oneself."

L'Amour had no use for those who say we have but one life to live. "For the one who reads, there is no limit to the number of lives that may be lived, for fiction, biography and history offer an inexhaustible number of lives." Billingsley summed up L'Amour's philosophy thusly, "In other words, books offer an education." I am in complete agreement.

> *All good books are alike in that they are truer than if they really happened and after you are finished reading one you will feel that it all happened to you, and afterwards it all belongs to you.*
>
> —ERNEST HEMINGWAY

In a recent letter, Dan, a friend from Texas, echoed L'Amour's thoughts on self-education: "You have the crux of the matter right there. Almost all education is, indeed, self-education. Teachers in a classroom are 'hucksters,' conning, cajoling, threatening; and all sorts of methods are employed to get the child to see a value in learning. Why do you and I learn? We want to." Dan, by the way, is a teacher in Houston.

Pursuing *your* personal education

What is it that *you* need to learn? Or want to learn? Perhaps you want to further your education because you hope to advance in your job. Obviously, you'll want to look for books, magazines, and periodicals that relate to your particular field: computers, electronics, sales, journalism, broadcasting, finance, public speaking, the beauty industry, cooking, gardening, or a specific trade. The list is endless. You'll get an excellent education through books and other writings, and the authors, your teachers, are masters in their fields. Best of all, you can learn at your own speed at a very reasonable rate.

Perhaps your need for education requires the hands-on kind of training found in how-to books; these can often supplement and overlap the aforementioned. Specific crafts such as jewelry, pottery, stained glass, metalwork, woodworking, basket weaving, dressmaking, and myriad others are covered in graphic detail in books. They're yours for the reading.

How-to books are not limited to the learning of crafts. One of the books that most profoundly affected my early life and philosophy was *How to Win Friends and Influence People* by Dale Carnegie. This book should be the bible for those who need training and guidance in the fine art of getting along with people in everyday business and social situations. I read it as a young, impressionable teenager and credit it to a great degree for whatever success I may have had in life, especially my experience in the world of broadcasting and time sales. Carnegie's sequel, *How to Stop Worrying and Start Living,* which deals with what is probably the greatest personal problem in the world today—worry—is another must-read. I am totally inspired every time I pick up one of Carnegie's books; they should be in every reader's personal library because they offer practical, tested formulas for solving many of life's difficult problems.

If you're a self-help junkie like me, you just want to be the very best you can be in every area of your life. You want to be a good parent, a good neighbor and responsible community leader, have loving relationships, be beautiful inside and out, and an all-around good person. Look to the self-help/psychology section of the library or your bookstore and begin your personal transformation process. It will be exciting!

Then there's the physical area of life: health, nutrition, exercise, and lifestyle. In books you'll find everything you need to know to transform your present physical existence from one of mediocrity and lethargy to a life of beauty, strength, and radiant good health.

How many a man has dated a new era in his life from the reading of a book.

—HENRY DAVID THOREAU

So, read a book. Read several. Start with one a month and increase to one a week. I often find myself reading two or more books simultaneously depending on my needs and mood. Get in the reading habit. Approach your reading with enthusiasm and anticipation. You'll find that books will become your friends, friends that you can always count on and turn to at any time of the day or night. As Martin E. Tupper said, *"A good book is the best of friends, the same today and forever."* When you're in a strange mood or state of ennui, need inspiration, motivation, or special advice, turn to one of your "friends." You will be rewarded a thousandfold. Books are marvelous companions, they're always there when you need them, and they never let you down. When you have books in your life, you'll never be lonely; books can be the best company you'll ever find.

> *Reading all the good books is like a conversation with the finest men of past centuries.*
>
> —RENÉ DESCARTES

If reading a book seems too time-consuming to you, read a newspaper, and read one daily. I know many people who are proud of the fact that they do not own a television and wouldn't watch one if they did. Often these are the same people who say they never read the daily paper. Perhaps they agree with Richard Brinsley Sheridan, who, in a previous century, said:

> *The newspapers! Sir, they are the most villainous—licentious—abdominable—infernal—not that I ever read them—no—I make it a rule never to look into a newspaper.*

But how in the world do such people know what's going on? In my opinion, reading a daily newspaper is an absolute must if you want to be, and sound, knowledgeable. Please, make the reading of one a daily habit. As Arthur Miller said in 1961, "A good newspaper, I suppose, is a nation talking to itself."

To sum up my thoughts about the value of reading, let me echo Logan Pearsall Smith, who said, "People say that life is the thing. But I prefer reading." Yes, Mother, I prefer reading!

Writing—the key to expressing yourself clearly

But I also enjoy writing, and so to my way of thinking, it's logical to look next to writing as a way of obeying Commandment II, Expand Your Mind. If you want to expand your mind, you must write. I don't mean you must write books, newspaper stories, or magazine articles, I mean you must *write*. You must learn to put your thoughts and ideas down on paper. Why? Because this is the only way to organize your mind, to train it, to actually make it put what you *think* into words. And that isn't always easy, my friends.

How many people in your personal life, and those you hear on radio and TV, frequently in the area of sports, say "you know?" endlessly? "You know," "I mean," "you know what I mean" are phrases repeated ad infinitum and ad nauseam by people being interviewed on so-called big-time shows as well as local media. By their constant "you knows," these personalities are trying to convey the thought that surely we understand what they're trying to say, but just can't. One way to begin to overcome this prevalent obstacle, which drives me up the wall, is to practice putting your thoughts on paper. If you know, *really* know, what you mean to say, it is not necessary to bombard your listeners or conversational partner with an ongoing barrage of "you knows."

Yes, the best way to eliminate those all-too-frequent "you-knows," which is only superseded in annoyance by the frequently used "like" which often precedes the infuriating "You know," such as "Like, you know, I mean . . ." a phrase which is bound to brand you as immature and naive is to put your thoughts in writing. Being able to write well and convey your ideas succinctly and intelligibly will clarify your thinking and move you rapidly to the head of the class, or the firm, so to speak. All too frequently, rather than diplomas, educational background, and IQ, the single highest criterion by which we're judged is the ability to communicate clearly our thoughts in writing, as well as out loud.

> *In a very real sense, the writer writes in order to teach himself, to understand himself; the publishing of his ideas, though it brings gratification, is a curious anticlimax.*
>
> —ALFRED KAZIN

My friend Hans was born in Germany. He came to the States at the age of fourteen which seems to be the definitive age when it comes to the retaining of accents. He tells me that if one is younger than fourteen when moving to a country with a different language, the original accent is overcome or lost. Over the age of fourteen, the accent remains, at least to a degree. He illustrates this by naming well-known actors, statesmen, and politicians who have accents, such as Henry Kissinger and Arnold Schwarzenegger. His theory appears to be true. Hans frequently laughs about his speaking and writing abilities; when making a slight mistake, he'll say jokingly, "What do you expect? English is my second language!"

Hans, being a true entrepreneur, started a company a couple of years ago called Discover Vietnam. He conducts bicycle and culinary tours of Vietnam, a country in which he lived and worked as an employee of the United States government during the war years beginning in 1968. Because Discover Vietnam is a one-man operation, Hans must do everything—from writing all brochures, flyers, promotional and PR material and arranging visas and transportation needs to greeting his tour members when they arrive in Vietnam and catering to their many whims and needs while there. In addition, he must cycle with them from one end of the country to the other.

In the beginning, his written material was rough in spots; it was apparent that English was his second language. Now, after much practice and many reams of paper, his brochures, flyers, and other mailers are flawless. With Hans, practice made perfect. It can do so for you as well.

"But why should I write?" you ask. "I'm not in the tour business; I have no need for brochures, flyers, and PR material." You may not have need for brochures, flyers, and the rest of it, but whatever your vocation or aspiration, you *do* have a need to express yourself adequately, to properly showcase your many attributes, which, unless clearly expressed, usually remain hidden.

> *To write is to write is to write is to write is to write is to write is to write is to write.*
>
> —GERTRUDE STEIN

If you feel like Gene Fowler, who said *"Writing is easy, all you do is sit staring at a blank sheet of paper until the drops of blood form on your forehead,"* let me suggest you buy a thesaurus. My copy of *Roget's Interna-*

tional Thesaurus is well-worn; the most-referred-to book in my personal library. It sits by my side daily as I write. At one time, I believed that if I had only one book to peruse for the rest of my life, it would be a thesaurus, because I am fascinated by words. With your trusty thesaurus by your side, you can eliminate those previously mentioned nerve-shattering meaningless "you knows" and "likes" from your speech and conversation.

If you still are uneasy about writing and don't know where to start, I suggest writing letters. To me, receiving a letter, a personal letter, is far better than receiving a bouquet of flowers or a box of candy. And the letter will not wilt or make me fat! It will be something that I can save, a keepsake that will continue to bring joy to my heart long after the day that it came in the mail. Write to your mother or sister, or your dad or brother, and then watch the surprised response. Or write to an old school buddy or a friend who has moved away. Write to say thank you for a gift or a favor, or to someone you care for, for just being. And if you're in love, what could be more meaningful than a sincere letter written to your one and only?

To those who say e-mail has replaced writing letters as a means of communication, I say, "No way!" and I'm sure Miss Manners will agree with me. Both have a place in our lives, e-mail for its immediacy, letters for their depth and longevity and, occasionally, their sentimental value. Can you wrap a batch of e-mail in pink ribbon and store it for posterity? I maintain a regular correspondence with several friends, some of whom I've never met. Often a letter to me will begin with warm feelings concerning the art of letter writing, as did this recent example from pen pal Bob J:

Thanks for your letter—I seldom receive personal correspondence, so it was most welcome. Perhaps the telephone has more or less eliminated the necessity for letter writing. I like to write letters, and do so frequently to friends and relatives, but do not often get many in return, especially not of the "meaty" type like yours. I might add that your good writing is in itself a pleasure to read. So much of what passes for writing these days is pedestrian and perfunctory at best.

If you want to get some writing practice in, and have no one else to write to, write to me; I will respond. You'll find my P.O. box at the back of this book.

Stand up and speak

One of the most effective ways of both communicating and expanding your mind is to be forced to stand up and speak. I say *forced* because most people will not willingly stand up in front of a group of people and expound their ideas. In fact, as we've all heard countless times, when it comes to fear, speaking in front of people takes precedence over the fear of death. But speaking in front of people makes you, *forces* you, to stop and think about what you want to, or must, say. That is, if you can actually *think* in such an unnerving position.

If you're in a job that requires you to address a group, regardless of size, and the prospect terrifies or intimidates you—emotions that affect almost everyone, regardless of fame, fortune, or station in life—I suggest you join Toastmasters. In a friendly, supportive atmosphere, the organization offers great training methods that are guaranteed to help you gain confidence and overcome shyness and embarrassment. I was a Toastmaster for many years and highly recommend them. The hands-on experience I received at every meeting definitely served to expand my mind. To this day I continue to attend the Old Timers annual meeting of Oakland's Merritt 539.

> *Talkativeness is one thing, speaking well is another.*
>
> —SOPHOCLES

Listen. You might learn something

No, I stand corrected. Listen, you *will* learn something! Listen to people. Ambrose Bierce said, "A bore is a person who talks when you wish him to listen." How true that is! And we are all guilty. How many times have you waited for that "bore" to shut up so that *you* could express your views? Remember that conversation is a two-way street; if you hope to be listened to, you must *listen* to your conversational partner so that you can make fitting comments and ask appropriate questions. Even if you simply nod and make appreciative noises such as "ah!", "oh?", and "uh-huh," you'll be thought of and remembered as a scintillating conversationalist!

> *The more the pleasures of the body fade away, the greater to me is the pleasure and charm of conversation.*
>
> —PLATO

Yes, conversation can offer both pleasure and charm. And if you listen carefully, you may also learn something.

One of the best methods of listening to learn is through audiotapes and CDs. To me, this is one of the easiest ways to learn almost anything, and my very favorite. I like listening to tapes and CDs because they allow me to do something productive with my mind when doing mundane chores around the house or yard, or while exercising, driving, or walking my dog. You can find tapes of every description and for every purpose in bookstores everywhere, as well as through catalogs.

My first book, *The Positive Thinker,* emphasized the benefits of listening to audiocassette tapes, particularly personalized tapes made by you, the reader. My Personal Power Plan, or PPP for short, was built around the concept of a personal tape that you make after determining your goals and desires in the six categories of life: mental, physical, spiritual, relationships, career-professional, and financial. I call my PPP plan a *personal* plan because you write it to fit your specific goals and desires, then you record it and listen to it daily; and a *power* plan because it works with powerful invisible forces. Your PPP *will* produce the future you desire *if* you follow the plan.

The three steps of the plan are as follows. First, you determine exactly what you want in every category of your life down to the smallest detail. Second, you write your life script to read the way you want your future to be. Finally, you personally record your script, utilizing affirmations and proven methods, including contemporary advertising principles used by the media. The end result becomes your Personal Power Plan. I made my original PPP tape in 1984 and listening to it has resulted in rich rewards in all categories of my life.

In addition, I occasionally make personal tapes for a variety of reasons and occasions, for my private listening, depending upon my need. Hearing one's voice on tape has a profound effect. I've used this method for purposes such as overcoming stage fright before an important speech, and to combat worrisome situations such as an exam, separation from a loved one, or a trip to the dentist. You might also want to consider making a personal tape for any number of compelling reasons.

Regarding the PPP and the effect of a personal tape, let me quote from a letter I just received from Dolores, who wrote to me after reading *The Positive Thinker:*

> *What I must tell you first because I'm so excited about it is that just a little while ago I made my PPP tape! I'm so proud of myself! It's 22 minutes long and I immediately sat down with my eyes closed and listened to it in its entirety. I was amazed at what a powerful effect it had on me. This is what I've been looking for. For years, I've written affirmations, over and over, which works very well, except that many times the time element becomes a problem. Also, I've journaled and written for so many years that I have an accumulation of notebooks that I periodically purge. The tape is the perfect way to handle the whole thing. It's an easy, simple way to accomplish a monumental job. It's the HEARING that makes the difference. And when I heard my own voice telling me what I've been hearing in my own head for so long—that was the brass ring!*

Listen—and learn a new language

Recently, I met a man who announced that he was a linguist. *Webster* says a linguist is a person accomplished in languages; one who speaks several languages. My new friend certainly met that qualification; he spoke seven languages fluently. Amazing; most of us are still trying to master English!

You may not wish to become a linguist, but if one of your ambitions is to learn just one new language, you can't beat the audiotape method. Hans is presently listening to two different audio approaches to the Vietnamese language, which, he tells me, is very difficult for a Westerner. With his taped lessons, he can actually hear the different inflections that are extremely meaningful in that language. Simple text could never adequately get that particular aspect across.

I took German lessons some years ago, prior to a visit to that country, from a private tutor and taped all of our sessions. Then I listened intently to the tapes while walking Charlie. Did I learn German? Not really. Because I was so embarrassed at my laughable attempts to express myself in what to me was a very difficult and guttural language, I really didn't try. Fortunately, I had Hans along to interpret for me, but if it were absolutely necessary that I learn German, I'd go back to my tapes, because, as Ludwig Wittgenstein said, "The limits of my language mean the limits of my world." For now, I'll stick with French, which comes much easier to me. *Parlez-vous français? Un peu? Très bien! Moi aussi.*

Take a course

I just spoke with Marty Nemko, who writes a weekly column entitled *Under the Radar* for the Sunday *San Francisco Examiner Chronicle*. Marty is a career coach; he has a regular radio show, and he's authored several books, including his latest, *Cool Careers for Dummies*. Last Sunday's column was entitled "Home Study Courses Boom," and I quote the short article in its entirety:

> Do you think of correspondence courses as those bogus programs on matchbook covers? Think again. Universities and other organizations now offer thousands of quality study-at-home courses on topics from aircraft mechanics to zoology. They use video or audiotape, on-line discussion groups, Web sites, and yes, plain old text. Check these on-line catalogs: www.lifelonglearning.com and America's Learning Exchange—the U.S. government's clearinghouse for training (www.alx.org). It claims that in a few years, it will be "*the* primary source of public knowledge about education and training resources."

If you're considering taking a course, don't limit yourself to correspondence courses, as excellent as they may be. Look into the adult-education courses available at your community high school or college and the many extension courses offered by various universities. If you want to learn, there are people and places waiting to teach you! Get on the mailing list of the learning institutions in your area. The course you take today may save your job tomorrow.

Learn firsthand from the experts

For receiving new information, or relearning old lessons, there is nothing like getting it "straight from the horse's mouth." For that reason I thoroughly enjoy the lectures, seminars, and workshops of people renowned in their fields. If I know that a famous author, or the authority on a subject of interest to me, will be appearing somewhere in my vicinity, you'd better believe that I'll be first in line for tickets. A lecture has the same effect on me as does attending a Broadway show and finally seeing and hearing what I've listened to and loved on tape, CD, or film. I literally get goose bumps when I see an idol in the flesh on stage or the platform. But not all speakers or seminar and workshop leaders are household names; most are simply experts in their fields, and deservedly so.

So, listen and learn from the experts. If you become passionate about a subject or field, you, too, can become an expert. I've heard countless times that a person can become a so-called expert if she's thoroughly and passionately studied a subject for five years; that length of time seems to be the key. My new friend Fred is an expert in bridge. Over the years, he's played in many countries and made a great deal of money doing so. As a result of her intense interest in newborn babies and the breastfeeding process, Beverly has become an instructor, author, and seminar leader on the subject, and a lactation consultant. And because David believes so strongly in the American dream of owning one's home free and clear, he has become an expert in the full sense of the word, advising potential homeowners, through his lectures, seminars, and books, on how to build their own home and own it free and clear in five years. What is it that turns you on? What do you think about all day? What would you rather read and talk about than anything else? The answers to these questions can lead you to your passion—and the discovery of your expertise. Think about it.

Pursue a hobby or favorite activity

One of Hans's favorite activities is cycling. He retired from his government job of thirty-some years to run marathons, but after many injuries and a couple of knee operations, he took up cycling. Easier on the body, he says. Cycling, and everything connected with the activity, became his passion. Then he visited Vietnam, where he had worked for our government during the war, and fell in love with that beautiful country. Somehow, it seemed a given that Hans, cycling, and Vietnam were destined to mesh, and as they say, the rest is history. Hans's tour company, Discover Vietnam, was born. Creating his own business definitely expanded Hans's mind; the expansion of his pocketbook will come later, hopefully!

In previous books, I've expounded on how my love of writing, especially letters, expanded to the writing of actual books—something I never would have believed possible a short ten years ago. And my friend Fern took her hobbies of jewelry making and pottery to new heights. She teaches classes in her crafts regularly through adult-education courses at local schools, and community park and recreation departments.

So yes, hobbies can expand your mind—and pocketbook! Think about your hobbies and favorite activities and explore the many ways they might be able to provide you with additional joy as well the bonus of an extra income. If you don't presently have a hobby that fits the qualifications, look into taking on new activities and learning new skills. You never know—what you learn today may end up being the bright spot in your future, or provide you with an incentive for retirement.

Volunteer—it can open new horizons!

I'm an active member of the National Speakers Association, and a few years ago, Sharon, also a member, called and asked if I'd help with the organization's annual summer speakers' school. She promised me that my responsibilities would be grunge work, so to speak; minor duties that she'd delegate.

We met a couple of times and I was glad to be the gofer, as the responsibilities of the entire project seemed overwhelming. Then one day my doorbell rang and Sharon was on my doorstep with a big box that contained all of the paperwork and files dealing with the project. Sharon tearfully announced that her mother was ill and she had to fly to New York to be with her and help for an indefinite period. She said everything I needed was in the box, and departed. I was now in charge!

Fortunately, the process had already commenced, a location was reserved, a banquet menu planned, and speakers engaged. But the rest was up to me. I had to deal with the advance mailing to thousands, reservations, table decorations, seating arrangements, sound systems, rest-room facilities, parking, and myriad other detail. In addition, there was the fifty-page workbook that became my total responsibility. One learns by doing and everything went off well—so well, in fact, that I found myself volunteering to chair the event the following year.

The following year found the organization in a tight financial squeeze; booking a high-cost hotel was out of the question. It was up to me to come up with a suitable facility of appropriate size and convenient location that would allow us to utilize accommodations that must include a large auditorium and classrooms at little or no cost. After many days and endless calls, I finally located a college campus that fit the bill. It did not have on-site audiovisual systems, so I had to seek them out, at low cost, and arrange for someone to operate the equipment. Then I had to find a caterer to provide vegetarian and nonvegetarian box lunches, coffee and other beverages at breaks, and a wine reception at the conclusion of the event. Of course, there were the usual mailings that accompany a large event of this nature, plus the planning, pricing, and publicity of same. Obviously, there was the actual program to consider, and the individuals who would be the stars of the show. And then there was the ever-important workbook! Coordinating the event and attending to every detail was a monumental effort, and everything went well—with only a glitch or two.

Expand my mind? You bet! I learned a lot and had much fun—plus a near–nervous breakdown on the side! But that particular exercise did a great deal for my self-confidence. I now know that I can stage a large event and have it come off successfully, because, as Virgil said, "Fortune sides with him who dares." In fact, I felt so confident that I offered to chair my next high-school reunion. Because of the monumental year our class would be celebrating, this would probably be our largest and most important reunion. I did not let the fact that I live in California and our reunion would be located in New Jersey deter me. Of course, I had enormous help from classmates back east, but still, I bore the responsibility of making many major decisions. I tend to agree with Napoléon Bonaparte, who said, "If you want a thing done well, do it yourself." What is it that you'd like to see done well? Consider volunteering to take over the job. It will expand your mind! And as a bonus, a project of this nature can also make a great addition to your résumé.

I share the stories of my experiences with these projects not to impress you with my competency or organizational skills, of which I have only an average amount. On the contrary, these were accomplishments that fall into the "I can do that!" category. The phrase "I can do that!" is a magic one about which I wrote an entire book. When faced with a challenge, large or small, it can overcome self-doubt and lack of confidence, and fan an invisible spark into a flame that will shine brightly, lighting the way to self-discovery, success, and fulfillment. The next time you're faced with a situation that puts you in a state of trepidation, state the powerful phrase "I can do that!" with confidence and watch the desired result come about as if by magic.

First say to yourself what you would be; and then do what you have to do.

—EPICTETUS, *Discourses*

Two rules for being and getting what you want

What is it that you would be? What is your dream? What excites you? What, as my friend, Connie, says "melts your butter"? Do you dream of being an actor or a singer? Writing a book or play? Learning a new language or instrument?

Rule number one is part of the "as if" portion of the Law of Expectation, which I explored in depth in *The Positive Thinker*. I hereby quote in brief: "The Law of Expectation says that what you expect and believe with confidence will tend to materialize. What you believe becomes your reality. You must act *as if* your expectation has already come to pass. And, because there is a definite causal link between belief and behavior, your expectations and belief determine your behavior." As Doug Hooper, author of *You Are What You Think,* said in a recent article: "This may seem far out but we live in a mental world and as the Bible says (Mark 11:24) we should pray believing we already have what we are praying for." So act "as if" what you want *is* an actuality. It soon will be so.

Rule number two follows through on the second part of the above quote from Epictetus: "Do what you have to do," or, as I discussed in Chapter 17 of *I Can Do That!,* "Do whatever it takes." If you do whatever it takes, or what you have to do, you *will* achieve your goal. This is a true case of cause and effect. If you do whatever it takes, you are instituting the *cause.* The *effect* is that you will achieve your goal. Knowing that you have the power to institute cause in your life, thereby bringing about the effect you desire, gives you total responsibility over your existence and future. Powerful stuff.

Often people do not want to acknowledge this responsibility. One of the many letters I received after writing *I Can Do That!* was from a woman who, even though she had no experience whatsoever, desired to be an actress on the New York stage or in Hollywood films. Her long letter cited many reasons why she could not do it: Her boss would not give her time off to attend auditions, she had no transportation from her suburban home into New York City to participate in the auditions even if she could swing the time off, and if she was selected, she would be unable to pay her bills until her name went up in lights, on and on. Then she said, "And don't suggest I look into community or Little Theater locally. I can't be bothered with that small-time stuff. I think I'm good enough to go straight to Broadway."

I wrote her a lengthy reply but never heard back. Basically, she was not doing whatever it took to achieve her dream; all she was doing was whining and complaining about the supposed obstacles in her way. Don't allow yourself to get caught in that trap. Do *whatever it takes* to make *your* dream become a reality. My prediction is that in years to come, this woman will join the "if-onlys," those who sigh about lost opportunities: "If only my boss had let me have an afternoon off to audition . . ." "If only someone had driven me into the city so I wouldn't have had to take public transportation . . ." "If only my bills would somehow have been miraculously paid until I was discovered and became a star . . ." If only she took responsibility for her life and dreams, if only she did whatever it takes, she might realize her dream or something close enough to it—such as being

the star in a local Little Theater production, for starters—
which could have been equally satisfying and actually
have paved her way to Broadway. I have never aspired
to be on the Broadway stage, but I can tell you that
applause from any audience, even that of a local play-
house, can be heady indeed!

The only limits in one's life are self-imposed.
—DR. DENIS WAITLEY

Do you need an attitude adjustment?

Perhaps, as Dr. Waitley states, you have personally
imposed limits on your life. And like the woman in the
previous example, you have done this through your attitude. Attitudes fall into two categories, positive and
negative, reflecting your personal mental position, feelings, and emotions toward life and all that happens to
you. Your attitude will also have a positive or negative
effect on all people you come into contact with. I covered this briefly in *Putting the Positive Thinker to Work*.
Because it bears repeating, I hereby do so:

Negative attitudes reflect anger, fear, hostility, dis-
respect, prejudice and intolerance. Other negative attitudes include arrogance, selfishness, lack of
confidence, and excessive defensiveness. They are all
destructive. On the other hand, positive attitudes reflect confidence, faith, hope, awareness, respect, cooperation, openness, mutual concern, and tolerance
among other things. Positive attitudes are always
constructive.

Your attitude is the "you" you present to the world. If you present a negative attitude, you will never succeed, you will never attain your goals, you will never create lasting friendships and associations. You will never be happy. However, if you present a positive attitude, you will attract all the things you want out of life: friends, success, fulfillment and, above all, happiness and peace of mind.

The greatest discovery of my generation is that a human being can alter his life by altering his attitude of mind

—WILLIAM JAMES

Doesn't it make sense to cultivate a positive attitude, a positive outlook on life? Doesn't it make sense to reprogram yourself with positives, thereby eliminating the negatives programmed into you by others? Doesn't it make sense to start now—today—to become a positive person—a happy, fulfilled, successful person? You can do it. Remember—you and you alone are in control of your thoughts.

There is a basic law that like attracts like. Negative thinking definitely attracts negative results. Conversely, if a person habitually thinks optimistically and hopefully, his positive thinking sets in motion creative forces—and success instead of eluding him flows toward him.

—NORMAN VINCENT PEALE

Monitor your thoughts

Yes, it's vitally important to remember that you are in control of your thoughts. You are the only thinker in your head. Under certain dire circumstances you may find yourself controlled by others, but under no circumstances can anyone control your thoughts; you and you alone are in control of what goes on in your mind.

The highest possible stage in moral culture is when we recognize that we ought to control our thoughts.

—CHARLES DARWIN

You must constantly monitor your thoughts. And that isn't always easy when, for the most part, we've been brought up in what is an essentially negative world. When negative, pessimistic thoughts, feelings, and emotions arise, we usually start to feel down, dissatisfied, lethargic, and uncomfortable. We find ourselves reverting back to those old negatives programmed into our minds since childhood: "You're stupid!" "I can't handle this; I'm gonna blow it." "I'm not good enough." And so on. That's when we have to bring out what I call the stoppers: Stop! Halt! Cancel! Say whichever stopper has the most power for you. Say it silently or aloud—shout if necessary. This is to get your personal undivided attention. That is important because you do not want these miserable "weeds"—for that is what they are to your mental garden—to take root in your mind. Then substitute the negative thought, feeling, or emotion with a positive affirmation. I suggest having several affirmations handy for such emergencies. Prepare them in advance, according to the rules for writing affirmations that were given in the previous chapter. For your convenience, I'll repeat the rules here:

Affirmations must be stated in the present tense.

They must be stated as if the result were an actuality.

Goals must be specific, not vague.

A feeling of gratitude, appreciation, or thankfulness must be present.

Experience the feeling or emotion accompanying the expected result.

I cannot adequately stress the importance of affirmations. The working title of my first book, *The Positive Thinker,* which dealt in a large part with affirmations, was *What You Say (to Yourself) Is What You Get.* Essentially, what I meant by that title is that we are what we think; the dialogue that goes on endlessly in our heads—what we *say* to ourselves—is what we get out of life. If our mental dialogue is negative, we attract negativity into our lives. Conversely, if our mental dialogue is positive, we attract positivity into our lives. The way to control our lives and ultimate destiny is through our thoughts. Properly worded affirmations are marvelous tools in the ongoing battle to help us change and control our thinking—and therefore change our lives and control our destinies.

Watch your thoughts; they become words.
Watch your words; they become actions.
Watch your actions; they become habits.
Watch your habits; they become character.
Watch your character; it becomes your destiny.

—FRANK OUTLAW

As we sum up Commandment II, Expand Your Mind—
and the complex of elements that compose the mind,
whatever they might be; nerve cells, dendrites, synapses,
and neural transmitters—remember the E-word: Expand.
Read, write, speak, attend seminars and workshops, take
and teach classes, volunteer, and all the rest of what
we've discussed. Take control of your thoughts, monitor
them, think positively, and utilize affirmations. Act "as
if," and do whatever it takes. As Horace said, "Rule your
mind or it will rule you."

My Resolutions

In regard to Commandment II, *Expand Your Mind,* these are my resolutions:

....

....

....

....

....

....

....

....

....

....

....

....

....

....

....

....

....

....

....

....

....

....

....

....

Nurture Your Spirit

Great men are they who see that spiritual is stronger than any material force, that thoughts rule the world.

—RALPH WALDO EMERSON

WHAT does spirit—or being spiritual—mean to you? For the past few weeks, knowing that I would soon write this chapter, I polled friends and some acquaintances on the subject of spirituality and what it means to them. Frequently, I got blank stares; other times, a mumbled reply followed by a quick change of subject. Or, as with one of my attempts to openly discuss what to me is an exciting dimension of human nature, although a surprisingly taboo subject to many, I was delivered a lengthy sermon on the spirit/soul versus the devil, the light side of human nature versus the dark, and the sad fact that the devil and darkness are, according to the speaker, apparently winning hands down. Sad to contemplate, and I don't believe it, but perhaps that's why some people say the world is quickly "going to hell in a handbasket."

Last week I had lunch with a retired psychologist who

was introduced to me because he claims to teach a course on spirituality at a prestigious Los Angeles University; I looked forward to a lively discussion. When I asked him the title of his class and his definition of spirituality, he refused to answer. He said, "Why should I tell you? I spent twenty years studying spirituality and I'm not going to tell you about my class or give you my definition. I suggest that if you aspire to write about it, you, too, spend twenty years in research and then come up with your own definition." While I was shocked at his uncharitable attitude, I noticed that he seemed flustered and embarrassed. Perhaps he found it difficult or uncomfortable to discuss such a personal matter as one's spiritual beliefs in a one-on-one situation rather than from the platform, and preferred to assume a stance of bravado and superiority instead.

I told him that at this stage of life I don't have twenty more years to spend on that project or any other, and that I had only asked for the definition I assumed he would give any student considering taking his course. Actually, I knew I could easily find an adequate answer through my faithful friend *Webster*, who, unlike the professor, does not worry about plagiarism. *Webster* says, "Spirit: the immaterial intelligent or sentient (capable of feeling) part of a person."

Lest you think I am a novice to the wonders and obvious confusion concerning spirit, spirituality, and soul, let me assure you that I have spent far more than the professor's twenty years—actually thirty-five-plus years—avidly reading and researching everything I could get my hands on concerning this fascinating and vitally important aspect of our lives. And I've merely touched the tip of the iceberg. Am I an expert, as he professed to be? Far from it; I'm merely a sincere and serious seeker, as are many of us who understand that the search is ongoing and endless.

My friend Pete, a roofing contractor who loved his job because he felt working on roofs allowed him to be close to God and the heavens, often asked, "When will I become enlightened, Alice?" I do not have the answer, of course, but to Pete I usually said something to the effect that, try as we may, none of us, regardless of our education, desire, and lifetime work, will ever totally know and understand spirituality, life's awesome complexities, and the reasons for our individual existence.

But I do have a definition of, or at least deep thoughts about, spirit/soul; I put the words together because I have trouble separating them. Algeron Charles Swinburne said something similar: "Body and spirit are twins: only God knows which are which." I'm inclined to agree that only God knows which are which; certainly I don't. So be forewarned; I may often use the two terms interchangeably.

One definition of spirit/soul

To me, your spirit/soul is the real you; your true essence; the You that existed before you were born and the You that will continue to live after your death, at least as we interpret the term. Your spirit/soul is your subconscious, your wise inner voice; the voice that guides you in determining true values and right from wrong; the voice that you can always count on regardless of outside forces. Your spirit/soul is your higher self; your direct line to God and the Kingdom within. Spirit is also your connection to nature and the magnificently beautiful, awesome external world in which we are privileged to live. Your spirit is part of the very spark that started with the Big Bang, thus commencing the chain of life; therefore you have a oneness with the universe. Your spirit/soul is the You that is You, now and for eternity.

He is immortal, not because he alone among creatures has an inexhaustible voice, but because he has a soul, a spirit capable of sacrifice and endurance.

—WILLIAM FAULKNER

To get back to my original question: "What does spirit and spirituality mean to you?" No doubt you have your own, personal definition. If not, now is a good time to start thinking about it because spirituality is vital to your life, happiness, and peace of mind. In the two previous chapters, we looked at the importance of taking care of your body and expanding your mind. Your spirit is part of the triad, the union of three: mind, body, and spirit. Each has equal significance and importance.

Ways of becoming spiritual

One of the first ways of becoming more spiritual is to cultivate the *desire* to become so. In order to cultivate the desire, you must *think* about becoming spiritual and what spirit/soul and spirituality mean to you. The obvious progression is to read, and as you read, you will become inspired, for, as Ralph Waldo Emerson said,

"Books are for nothing but to inspire." This will naturally lead you to search for additional information on the subject.

Next, I suggest you initiate conversations about spirit/soul and spirituality, as I attempted to do prior to starting this chapter. This will lead to all sorts of stimulating conversations as well as surprising confrontations and unusual outcomes. I use those words because that was how I felt after my two conversations mentioned above. I never expected my good friend to deliver such a serious, depressing sermon, nor did I expect the retired psychologist to be so confrontational. In retrospect, both encounters were interesting and enlightening, perhaps educational as well, if for nothing more than learning about people and their opinions.

> *Where there is much desire to learn, there of necessity will be much arguing, much writing, many opinions; for opinion in good men is but knowledge in the making.*
>
> —JOHN MILTON

After you've done some reading or other research, and had conversations or prompted others to speak their thoughts, I suggest you spend some time with pen in hand and put your personal ideas and feelings on the subject down on paper or in a private journal. This might take some time; after all, this is a serious matter. Don't be tempted to skip this vital exercise. When you've completed it, you'll realize the value and importance of clarifying your thoughts on this vital aspect of your life.

A personal, meaningful, spiritual experience

Because we're working on this together, I'd like to share two very personal, meaningful spiritual experiences with you. The first happened many years ago. I was "on the path," which was a prevalent term at that time, but I never considered myself religious or even spiritual, and so did not ever expect to have a "meaningful experience" in what might be considered the religious sense.

I was visiting Jackie, a friend who refurbished houses in the beautiful, exclusive Carmel/Monterey area of California. Jackie had just finished a house that she had been working on for months. Prior to putting it up for sale, she invited me to visit and enjoy the peaceful setting for a few days. Her delapidated fixer-upper had been turned into a lovely cottage, charming and homey, everyone's dream hideaway.

On the first night of my stay, I was sound asleep in one of Jackie's three elegantly decorated bedrooms when I was suddenly awakened by a voice. It said, "You have a friend in Jesus." The voice spoke in English, without any accent whatsoever; actually, it sounded very American. I sat up in bed and said, "What? What did you say?" The voice repeated exactly what it said the first time; "You have a friend in Jesus." This was not a dream; when I questioned the voice, I was wide-awake. I am certain that the voice I heard was real.

I was amazed and perplexed; astounded, actually. Although a supposed Christian, I had never spent much time thinking about Jesus. So, when a voice came to me in the middle of the night, telling me that I had a friend in Jesus, I was stunned. What interested me most of all was that the voice had uttered the word "friend." It did not say, "Jesus is your savior" or any of the standard salvation phrases; it said simply, "You have a *friend* in Jesus."

A friend. Everyone needs a friend. What better friend than Jesus! These were some of the thoughts that ran through my mind. And I will tell you that the same phrases run through my mind today. I truly, totally, and completely believe that the voice and his message—for the voice was a male voice—were sincere. I believe that I have a friend in Jesus. This has made a tremendous difference in my life. Having a true friend to turn to in all of life's travails is a wonderfully comforting thing. Without any embarrassment or feeling of intrusion, I readily turn to Jesus because I *know,* because I have been told, that He is my friend.

> *A true friend is the most precious of all posses-*
> *sions and the one we take the least thought*
> *about acquiring.*
>
> —LA ROCHEFOUCAULD

Although it was years before I shared this experience with anyone for fear of ridicule, I readily share this with you, dear reader, because I look upon you as a friend as well. I will tell you of my other moving experience shortly, but first, let us look into meditation as another means of becoming more spiritual.

Some thoughts on meditation

It is said that meditation calms nerves, relaxes the body, relieves tension and anxiety, releases energies, erases worry, reduces stress, and regulates heartbeat and blood pressure. And that's just for starters.

In addition, meditation opens the mind, stimulates creativity, promotes insight, increases awareness and higher levels of consciousness, enhances peace of mind, and helps us connect with God.

If meditation isn't an all-around panacea, I don't know what is! If only it could cure the common cold, curl your hair, prevent cavities, remove wrinkles, and reduce hips and thighs, we'd hardly need anything else!

Seriously, meditation is a healing force extraordinaire, available to each and every one of us free of charge. Not only does it cost nothing, it requires no special equipment, knowledge, educational requirements, or degrees. It is a nontoxic approach to a new way of life. All it takes is fifteen to twenty minutes of quiet time once or twice a day.

I first turned to meditation back in the mid-seventies when I was going through a difficult time, both in my personal and professional lives. A long-term relationship had terminated, and during that tumultuous time, I accepted a "job that I couldn't refuse"—a position that offered a significantly higher salary and more prestige. This meant giving up managing the radio stations I loved and that had become my life. I stupidly let dollar bills and grandiose titles conquer love and loyalty. As Fiorello La Guardia said, referring to a bad political appointment, "When I make a mistake, it's a beaut!"

The only one who makes no mistakes is one who never does anything.

—THEODORE ROOSEVELT

When my life seemed to be going down the tubes at a rapid rate, I panicked. I had heard of TM, Transcendental Meditation, and its benefits, and thought, hoped, prayed that it could help. I signed up immediately, and although I tried, sincerely, to learn, I was too uptight and distraught to relax enough to allow the program to produce the benefits promised. Instead, I turned to affirmations, something equally new to me, and found they had a beneficial effect.

But I did not discard meditation, nor should you. Over the years, I experimented with other forms of meditation but just couldn't seem to get over the how-to-do-it hurdle. Actually, it turns out, there's no how-to needed; you just "do it." More importantly, you must stick with it. There are many approaches, including focusing on a visual point such as a candle, measuring your breath, and repeating your mantra.

The idea is to sit still in a comfortable position, close your eyes, relax your muscles, calm the mind, and tame those racing thoughts. Impossible, of course. Because you *cannot* tame those racing thoughts, you must learn to ignore them, or control them the best you can.

Breathe slowly and naturally and repeat your mantra, focus word or chosen phrase. In the seventies, mantras were very "in." Everyone had to have one, and the one given you was absolutely secret, not to be repeated to anyone. If for some reason you forgot it, a special call was put into Maharishi Mahesh Yogi, the founder of TM, for supposedly he was the only one who knew of each and every mantra, or so I was told. More practical focus words or phrases include "peace," "one," "the Lord is my shepherd," "God is with me," or any personal meaningful word or phrase.

Assume a passive attitude. When thoughts come to mind, as they are bound to, ignore them. Gently return to the repetition of your mantra, word, or phrase. Above all, do not get uptight about the process and don't worry about whether it's working. It is, even if it doesn't seem so.

And like the age-old prescription for aspirin—"Take two and call me in the morning"—so it is with meditation; "Practice twice a day and continue forever," is the prescription. Or at least continue indefinitely. If you are tempted to give up, go back to the beginning of this commentary about meditation and reread the benefits.

For more information on meditation and how to do it, I recommend *The Relaxation Response* by Herbert Benson, M.D., and *How to Meditate* by Lawrence LeShan.

The maverick meditator

In many of the things I've done in life, I've been called a maverick. *Webster* says a maverick is "an independent individual who refuses to conform." It's not that I *refuse* to conform, it's just that I often see what appears to me to be a different or better way.

In regard to meditation, I thought there must be a better way—at least for me. When I tried to do it in the traditional manner, I had problems. One was the phone. Yes, you are supposed to turn off your phone. But I have seven extensions on my private phone line, and there are two other business phone lines coming into my house as well. I could not imagine turning off all the important expected calls, or relegating them to an answering machine. Unlike many, I am simply a person who cannot ignore a ringing telephone.

Then there is Charlie, my canine love. Charlie is the best, most sincere guard dog in the universe. Charlie barks or becomes agitated when the wind blows, the house creaks, or when he detects an animal entering our yard. He barks at squirrels, birds, butterflies, cats, other dogs, airplanes, helicopters, buses, and anything else that moves or breathes, including the gardener and meter reader. He is especially vocal around unleashed dogs; envious, probably! Trying to meditate when Charlie is in the house or on the premises is simply impossible.

Well, Dale Carnegie said something to the effect that "If you're given a lemon, make lemonade," and I thought to myself, "Of course! Charlie and I can work out this meditation thing." And we did, through our evening walks. I walk Charlie along our accustomed route every evening for fifty minutes, rain or shine, and have for ten years. I know the route so well, I do not need to concentrate on the sidewalk, bumps in the road, cross streets, and all the rest of it. My mind is free. Of course Charlie is doing his noisy thing, but there are also interludes of quietness. These interludes have become precious times of meditation for me. I think I can say that I have written—or at least formed the concepts for— many book chapters while on Charlie walks. Most of *The Positive Thinker* came to me while walking with him.

I tell you this because if you, too, feel that you are a maverick, that you simply can't meditate in the traditional manner, there may be a solution. It's up to you to find the solution that will work for you. I'm sure there are many.

More Charlie-walk observations

Walking Charlie can be a drag; often I wish I could renege but I never, *never* do; our daily walks are vital to both of our lives. And a commitment is a commitment. I am totally committed to Charlie and our mutual need for exercise—and mine for meditation! I know that I am more attuned to nature and all its wonders because of my daily walks. I marvel at birds, squirrels, and other living things, including humans; blue skies, white clouds, rainbows, and extravagant sunsets; exotic plants, brilliantly hued flowers, and the ever-changing trees along our route.

> *I think that I shall never see*
> *a poem as lovely as a tree . . .*
> *Poems are made by fools like me,*
> *but only God can make a tree.*
>
> **—JOYCE KILMER**

Kilmer's poem sums it all up; and yes, only God can make a tree. I have two favorites along my route. At the moment, in mid-December, both are totally barren and brittle looking; there seems to be no life left in their leafless branches. One, a nondescript growth that I'm sure no one else takes note of, has what I call its "once-a-year day," a phrase from a song in the musical *The Pajama Game*. Once a year, and only for a day or two, this anonymous tree presents an absolutely breathtaking canopy of pure white blossoms that completely cover the sidewalk. The first time I saw this floral extravaganza, I was stunned. As the old saying goes, I thought I had died and gone to heaven!

My other favorite is a persimmon tree. Every year, it gives me the greatest pleasure to watch this bleak, lifeless-looking growth along my path go from its hibernation of nothingness, through the many stages of transformation, to become a vibrant, beautiful carrier of succulent orange-colored fruit. Watching the evolution of these two special trees has gifted me with a personal kind of inner spirituality and peace.

Perhaps this is an appropriate time to tell you of my other spiritual experience, previously alluded to, which, coincidentally, includes a flowering bush or tree, this time a camellia.

God, prayer, and the camellia bush

It was about twelve years ago. My dad, who was close to ninety, was diagnosed with cancer. Somehow, even at his advanced age, I could not believe his case was terminal. I was certain he could overcome the disease and live until ninety-five, at least. Naturally, I prayed nightly, and earnestly, for his recovery.

At the same time, I was having some major renovation work done on my home, which included installing a deck as well as French doors from two of the downstairs rooms that would lead out to the proposed deck. The project required that one of my beautiful camellia bushes be transplanted so that one of the newly installed French doors could open without hitting it.

I called a man who was an expert on camellias, which I was told do not take kindly to transplanting. We arranged that he would supervise the uprooting and transplanting of the camellia; and the workmen were advised not to touch the bush prior to his arrival. He was due at noon, but at eight A.M. and to my horror, I found that the men had yanked the bush from the ground and tossed it to the side of the yard. The major portion of the root system had been left in the ground, not carefully unearthed according to the rules laid down by the transplant expert. I immediately called him to tell of the mishap, and he was so angry with both the workmen and me that he refused to come to see if the damage could be minimized. He did say, however, that I should cut back all leaves and foliage prior to the futile task of putting the abused, almost rootless plant back in the ground, which I did.

I then placed the poor shorn, bedraggled-looking camellia into the claylike soil—and digging the hole was no easy job, I'll tell you—which I carefully fertilized according to directions from both the expert and my nursery people.

I was quite upset. Here was a beautiful, healthy, living camellia bush in full bloom, and because I had decided to build a deck and install French doors, it was seriously harmed. So, nightly, when I prayed for my dad, I always added a postscript to God: "And please, dear God, let my camellia bush live, too. Forgive me for allowing harm to come to it."

Sadly, the transplanting did not take; the remaining leaves dropped off, the branches became brittle and broke, and finally, because the bush looked so pathetic and I didn't want to be reminded of my participation in its demise, I asked Hans to saw it off close to the ground—the only course we could take because the soil was so hard that it was impossible to simply pull it out.

Shortly thereafter, I received the dreaded call from New Jersey. On my return flight, after the funeral, I had much time to think, and at an altitude of thirty thousand feet, I had a conversation with God. It became very important to me that I know that my dad's spirit and soul lived on, that he was not "simply gone," and that's all there had been to his life. I begged God, upon my return, to give me a sign of some sort, something that I would know and understand beyond a shadow of a doubt, that, indeed, Dad was alive and well in a better place.

I had been home a couple of days, maybe a week. Hans was working in the yard. Suddenly he shouted to me, "Alice! Come out here this minute. Come and look!" I raced out to where he was standing in front of what I thought was the sawed-off, dead camellia bush. There, to my amazement, was a perfectly formed, miniature camellia bush about a foot in height, complete with exquisite white blossoms.

A sign? I have no doubt. What more perfect message could I have possibly received as a result of my prayers for my dad and the camellia, and my request for proof of an ongoing life for my dad, than a reincarnated camellia bush? Yes, I am a true believer. For those who might question, I will explain that upon examination, it turned out that the camellia's rebirth was the result of a tiny root that emanated from the top of the sawed-off, seemingly dead bush. In no way did someone simply place a new camellia where the old one had stood. More importantly, no one knew of my prayer and pleas to God for a sign.

Some thoughts on prayer

When I was a child and, later, a young girl, I went to Sunday school regularly with my good friend Gloria.

Often, after Sunday school, we attended the eleven o'clock church services with our parents. I don't really know about Gloria, but I was usually pretty squirmy during the services. Most of the sermons didn't make much sense, and often they had a frightening tone.

> *There is perhaps no greater hardship at present inflicted on mankind in civilized and free countries than the necessity of listening to sermons.*
>
> —ANTHONY TROLLOPE

But when the minister said, "Let us pray," I, of course, bowed my head with the rest of the congregation. Prayer at that time, considering my emotional and intellectual level, was "heavy." The pastor or minister talked in somber tones about our sins and hopes for salvation. Although I didn't know what I had done wrong, I was truly afraid of going to hell. As far as prayer was concerned, I think that early exposure got me off on the wrong foot.

Long before that, however, I was brought up on prayer, both at home and at school.

> *Now I lay me down to sleep*
> *I pray the Lord my soul to keep.*
> *If I should die before I wake*
> *I pray the Lord my soul to take.*
>
> —CHILDREN'S PRAYER

That prayer scared the daylights out of me. Every time I got to "If I should die before I wake," my little mind went into a state of panic. What did it mean to "die before I wake"? What did it *really* mean to die? What would happen to me? Where would I go or be? Actually, as adults, we all face some of those same questions, don't we?

In school, prayer was not only condoned, it was mandatory. We said the Lord's Prayer daily at the beginning of each schoolday, and that was followed by the Pledge of Allegiance. No separation of church and state in those days!

> *Our Father, which art in heaven, hallowed be thy name. Thy kingdom come. Thy will be done, on earth as it is in heaven. Give us this day our daily bread. And forgive us our trespasses, as we forgive those that trespass against us. And lead us not into temptation; but deliver us from evil: For thine is the kingdom, the power, and the glory, for ever and ever.*
> *Amen.*

As children, we all memorized this prayer and said it by rote, perhaps not really paying attention to or even vaguely understanding its meaning. This bothered me as a mature adult and I spent time seriously trying to decipher what, according to what I had been told, was the principal Christian prayer taught by Jesus to His disciples. For you, who may have similar concerns, I suggest you peruse chapter 2 of *Power Through Constructive Thinking* by Emmet Fox. Even though Fox has a reasonable explanation for the baffling phrase "lead us not into temptation," those words still continue to be a stumbling block for me.

> *I generally avoid temptation unless I can't resist it.*
>
> —MAE WEST

Perhaps a lighter approach to your personal prayer might be appropriate; by that I mean that you might consider addressing it in a manner more comfortable to you, one that is not threatening as was the minister's to me when I was a child.

Norman Vincent Peale, in *Power Thoughts for the Positive Thinker,* suggests you utilize minute prayers: "Pray as you go about the business of the day. Utilize minute prayers by closing your eyes to shut out the world and concentrating briefly on God's presence. The more you do this every day, the nearer you will feel God's presence."

In regard to God's presence, I came across this phrase some time ago and it has had a powerful effect on me: "I am now in the presence of God." Say this to yourself frequently throughout the day and tune into its meaning. I like to say it when I am on the street, in a crowded bus, standing in line, or on my walk with Charlie. "I am now in the presence of God." Wow! You can even say it when you are alone in your room, because the presence of God is there, with you, even if there are no others present. In addition, your room, or any room, is filled with things that were originally ideas; things and ideas that were created by people. All these things and ideas came from the Universal Mind from which everything emanates. No matter where you are or who you are with, say, "I am in the presence of God," and let the realization of its meaning strike you with full force.

Then you might like to have a conversation with God. As Clement of Alexandria said in *Stromateis,* "Prayer is a conversation with God." It took me a long time to understand that that's what sincere prayer can actually be: a conversation. It does not have to be a somber, frightening message delivered by a minister or pastor in sonorous tones, or a formal prayer that you might not quite understand. It can be a simple conversation much like one you might have with a dear friend or loved one.

Some time ago a friend gifted me with a subscription to *Daily Word,* a publication of Unity School of Christianity. One of the daily messages, dated March 31, 1996, and entitled "In the silence of prayer, God speaks to me" reads in part:

> I am always here for you because I love you, and I will always listen to you.

> Talk with Me and tell me what is on your mind and heart.

> Lean on Me, and know that I will support you through every experience in life.

> Call on Me whenever you feel lonely, whenever you need Me, and I will fill your heart with peace.

> I am a living, loving presence in your life, so let Me live and love through you. You will be blessed and be a blessing to others.

> Talk with Me at any time during the day or night and tell me your hopes and desires. You are My beloved child, and I care about you.

> Know that we are one in spirit and faith—now and always.

I like that message; I keep it by my bedside and refer to it frequently. For me, it takes the onus out of the structured, formal prayer that many of us think is the only appropriate way, and encourages me to converse with God in everyday language. I read this message nightly before I retire, along with one from Norman Vincent Peale's booklet, "How to Have a Good Day Every Day": "God watches over me, over my house, over all my loved ones. In His peace I have peace." This affirmation, which covers my major concerns, allows me to go to sleep in peace.

> *You pray in your distress and in your need;*
> *would that you might also pray in the fullness*
> *of your joy and in your days of abundance.*
>
> —KAHLIL GIBRAN

Yes, yes, *yes*! When you pray, never ever forget to thank God for your many blessings and the richness and abundance in your life.

The importance of faith

According to H. L. Mencken, "Faith may be defined briefly as illogical belief in the occurrence of the improbable." On the other hand, Samuel Butler said, "You can do very little with faith, but you can do nothing without it."

What does faith mean to you? The word "faith" is often used interchangeably with the word "religion"—especially in cases where there is less emphasis on institutionalized tradition and more on devoted adherence, such as the Christian *faith* or the Jewish *faith*. In another instance, "faith" is frequently used interchangeably with "trust"—both words denote the greatest degree of conviction that a person or thing will not fail in loyalty, duty, or service. Actually, faith is an intensification of trust, suggesting an even deeper conviction of fidelity and integrity, often in spite of no evidence whatever or even in the face of contrary evidence. In the Bible, Paul tells us, "Faith is the substance of a thing hoped for, the evidence of a thing unseen."

In her book *Key to Yourself,* Dr. Venice Bloodworth analyzes Paul's statement:

> Give that a moment's thought—Faith is the SUBSTANCE, the actual substance of anything we desire. The reason we have not demonstrated more faith is because of our lack of understanding. We have not understood that everything works in exact accord with a definite law. We must build our desires in our world within, build them in faith, hope, courage, and hold them regardless of outside appearance. Pay no attention to appearance. Your success, your happiness, and your health are all of your own making, and if you are not happy with conditions as they are you have only to visualize them as you would have them be in order to change them.

Unless you believe, you shall not understand.

—ISAIAH 7:9

Bloodworth goes on to say, "Because the power of the Universal Mind is invisible is no reason to doubt it."

How true that is! Following Bloodworth's trend of thought, we cannot see life except as a motive power; neither can we see spirit or soul. Love is invisible but we all believe in its power; and we can only see the effects of health, happiness, and peace of mind. Faith, too, is invisible, for it is, as Paul said, "the substance of a thing hoped for, the evidence of a thing unseen."

Belief becomes reality

So, it is vitally important for all of us to "keep the faith." By that I mean you simply have to *believe*—and believe totally. Why? Because what you believe becomes your reality. If you have a firm conviction about yourself and take it to be true and honest—that is, you *believe* it—it will become a real event in your life. That conviction will be reflected in the state of your affairs. It *will* become a reality. Your belief *is* your reality.

Nurture your spirit, my dear friends. Desire more spirituality. Think about it. Talk about it. Meditate. Pray. Have faith. And, above all, *believe*.

My Resolutions

In regard to Commandment III, *Nurture Your Spirit,* these are my resolutions:

....
....
....
....
....
....
....
....
....
....
....
....
....
....
....
....

....
....
....
....
....
....
....
....

Be Responsible and Trustworthy in All Ways

To be a man is, precisely, to be responsible.

—ANTOINE DE SAINT-EXUPÉRY

BE responsible. Exactly what does that mean? *Webster* says it means to take responsibility, either blame or credit, for one's conduct and obligations; to be trustworthy. S. I. Hayakawa, my favorite semanticist, says "responsible refers to the agreement by which one takes on the blame or credit of an endeavor over which one has charge. Being responsible," according to Hayakawa, "goes beyond this to anyone who is mature or able enough to discharge difficult or exacting duties, to delegate authority wisely, and to perform capably despite unforeseen obstacles."

In examining the structure of the word, it seems that responsibility could also be defined as the "ability to respond" to the many life situations and challenges that we all face daily.

What is your ability to respond to life's daily happenings? Do you willingly accept blame or credit—mentioned by both *Webster* and Hayakawa—where and when blame or credit are due? Obviously, we are all happy and more than willing to take the credit when everything goes well, but blame? Forget it! Most of us can always find other people, situations, and circumstances to blame when things go wrong.

The blame game

We can start at the beginning and blame our parents and the environment into which we were born; we can blame our gender, age, or appearance; we can blame our color, race, or religion—and that's just for starters. Don't forget the ongoing blame heaped upon the government, politicians, the bureaucracy, and the system in general. The weather, Mother Nature, and God, especially, always receive their fair share of blame. Some people even go so far as to blame the planets, moon, and stars for their personal state of affairs. If that's not enough, there's the ever-popular "the devil made me do it"!

Enough already! Knock it off. Grow up. Quit the blame game. Blamers are not mature, and they will never mature because they are not in touch with reality. When blaming ends, growth begins. Get out of the blame-game rut by becoming an *accepter*, an accepter of responsibility instead of a blamer. Accept responsibility for your actions, reactions, attitudes, thoughts, feelings, emotions, and conduct. In other words, accept responsibility—*full* responsibility—for your life and the way that you live it.

That's far easier said than done, of course. Although we may not realize it, we have all been programmed since birth by the many influential people in our lives: parents, siblings, relatives, peers, teachers, religious leaders, bosses, and coworkers; actually everyone with whom we have come in contact over the years. We react to the things that happen to us in predictable ways, because that's the way we've observed others, been taught, or habitually performed. Like it or not, we all too often are held captive by our habits. Or by our perceptions. If you examine your emotions, you'll discover that a perception is at the heart of every emotion, and our emotions cause our reactions; reactions that often become habitual.

Are you an actor or a reactor?

But that doesn't mean our reactions have been right in the past. In fact, if you relive some experiences, especially those in which you know you acted badly, you will see that you were a *reactor*. As a mature, responsible individual, it is important to become an *actor,* a person who does not let others decide how he will act, rather than a *re*actor, one who simply reacts to past programming or input.

It has been said that self-knowledge is the pinnacle of wisdom. But if we're always in a blame state, we'll never learn, never mature. Blamers' lives are on hold. Only you can know yourself; only you can change yourself. Therefore, it's important that we analyze our actions, ask ourselves why we do the things we do. It is important that we take personal responsibility—*full* personal responsibility—for our lives.

One way to do that is to accept that we, as individuals, are in charge of our lives and actions, not "them," the people we've blamed in the past. When change seems difficult, and change is *always* difficult, I like utilizing the "as if" concept, which I have written about frequently in the past. Acting "as if" is part of the Law of Expectation. When you act as if something is going to happen, you *expect* it to happen, you believe it will happen. Therefore, if you respond or act "as if" you are the person you wish to be, eventually *you will become that person*. An actor is a person who acts "as if."

Decide *now* to become an actor rather than a reactor. Decide now to make personal, responsible decisions about the appropriate way to act in all situations.

That's one of the most important realizations and accomplishments in life: to be an actor, not a reactor.

—SYDNEY HARRIS

Responsibility in one's personal affairs

Dan and Janine moved in together after both graduated from college. Janine found employment right away; Dan just couldn't seem to find the right job. Janine willingly paid the household bills, confident that Dan would pay his fair share when the right position presented itself. Nothing materialized, so Dan signed up for a variety of courses to increase his chances in the job market. After a couple of years, he found what seemed to be an appropriate position. Janine was relieved that Dan finally agreed to commence paying the utility and phone bills every other month.

Things went well for the first few months. Then one

day, the power was shut off and the telephone disconnected. It had been Dan's month to pay the bills. Apologizing profusely, Dan swore it would never happen again. But it did happen again, six months later. Janine was forgiving, but upset; because the phone and utilities were in her name, she feared for her credit rating.

The next Christmas, Janine gave Dan the stereo components he had been wanting. Dan gave Janine a large-screen TV, the better to see the sports events *he* avidly pursued. One night, some months later, the bell rang during the dinner hour. Janine answered to find two very large men at the door; there was a truck at the front curb. "We've come to pick up the TV," they informed her. "There have been no payments since the initial down payment."

Janine was furious with Dan. "After all our talks about responsibility and your empty promises! How could you be so negligent? I'm really going to have to give some serious thought to this relationship."

Janine paid the balance on the TV, so it was not carted off in the middle of Dan's ball game. And she did give serious thought to the relationship. It continued for a while, but the harm had been done. Janine said she simply could not plan the rest of her life around a man who was so totally irresponsible. The constantly postponed marriage date was canceled permanently and Dan eventually found himself looking for new quarters and a new partner.

Trust, like the soul, never returns once it is gone.

—PUBLILIUS SYRUS

Be worthy of trust

Yes, to be responsible is to be trustworthy, to be "worthy of trust." In the early days of computers, my friend Fred, with whom I worked, told me of his dreams and plans to start his own company based on the many new advances in the electronics industry.

Fred requested my help in writing his business proposal; that's how I became knowledgeable about his project. Fred required financial backing, start-up money to get the plan off the ground. His application was rejected by the Small Business Administration, so he turned to friends and relatives for funds. These mostly blue-collar, middle-class people from a small midwestern town joyfully got on Fred's bandwagon and invested in grand style.

Time went by; I was involved in my own career and temporarily forgot about Fred's entrepreneurial plan until I heard that a group of friends and relatives of his were coming to our area for a visit. Because Fred was a good friend and his quarters were inadequate, I offered to host a small party in my home for his visitors. The first and major question on everyone's mind was, "How is 'our' new business going, Fred?" Fred was evasive. I instantly realized, in horror, that he had dropped the ball. He had accepted the money from his trusting friends and relatives and had nothing to show for it.

I do not believe that Fred had any intention to defraud when he put his dream into motion, it's just that he didn't follow through in an honorable, responsible, and trustworthy fashion. Somehow he got bogged down, couldn't swing the project, and by neglect, lack of interest, and follow-through, or who knows what, he just let it die. But he could not bring himself to tell his investors of the status of "their company."

What I remember of that evening is the universal look of astonishment—and then betrayal—on the faces of Fred's friends and relatives. I exited to the kitchen and the welcome distraction of dishes and cleanup in order to avoid the disillusionment of those present. "But we trusted you," was the comment I heard most frequently stated from my kitchen retreat.

> *The holy passion of friendship is so sweet and steady and loyal and enduring in nature that it will last through a whole lifetime, if not asked to lend money.*
>
> —MARK TWAIN

At the end of my second book, *I Can Do That!,* I gave my post-office-box number and invited readers to correspond with me. I was extremely gratified by the response. Many had praise for the book. I assume that if a writer asks for input in the manner that I did, and someone takes the time to comply, the input will tend to be positive. Others told me how my personal story and the stories of others in the book inspired them to pursue their own dreams and goals. That pleased me because it was my intention to inspire my readers to action. Some correspondents were frustrated, however, that their life situations, for one reason or the other, did not allow them to "do that"—get out of their personal ruts, let alone achieve their goals. Their letters to me were of the "I dare you to find a solution to my problem" category.

I answered all of the letters. To the "I dare you's," I offered what I thought were reasonable ways for each writer to overcome her individual obstacles and realize her goals and desires. For the most part, I did not hear back from the letter writers, although I invited them to keep me posted on their progress.

One woman who became a regular correspondent, however, dared me also, in a way. Her letter began: "I know you won't read this letter, much less respond. I bet I'll never hear from you." She went on to say that she came from a dysfunctional family. My reaction to that statement, a frequent one in the letters I received, was to ruefully smile and say to myself, "Don't we all?"

Ellen (not her real name) told me she had dreams of becoming a writer and, in subsequent correspondence, sent me samples of her work. I find it difficult to judge or critique another's writing, but I did want to encourage her, as I do all aspiring writers. One of the problems with her submissions was that she wrote in a barely legible scrawl, often in pencil; there were many misspellings, and she used scraps of paper torn from notebooks and partially used stationery. In addition, her pages were often stained with coffee-cup rings and sticky fingerprints. Still, she wanted me to "get her published."

I suggested she go to the library or her local bookstore and read up on the proper ways to submit material to prospective publishers. She could not be bothered. I emphasized that editors and publishers had basic criteria for submissions: for starters, manuscripts and other material must be typed, double-spaced, on 8½-by-11-inch white paper. Ellen said she couldn't type and didn't care to learn. I never learned how to type either, in a formal way, but I have managed over the years, just like millions of other people.

Are you getting the picture that Ellen refused to accept personal responsibility for her dreams of becoming a publisher author? I realized this early on, of course, but continued to encourage. If she refused to type and persisted in writing in longhand, I suggested that she do just that—write in longhand, have her young daughter illustrate the stories to the best of her ability, then Xerox and put the material in presentation folders available at stationery stores, or have it bound at a copy place near her. I felt there could be a local audience for her stories presented in that form. Because they were basically targeted at young children, I suggested that she offer her stories in booklet form to children's hospitals, Sunday schools, and elementary-school students. The outcome was that she was angry with me for not "getting her published" and supplementing her income, and she told me that I fell down on the job of being her mentor.

In discussing this type of thing with other authors, I've been told by many that it is useless to become involved with one's readers and that they, as authors, make it a rule not to respond to correspondence. I disagree. If my words and encouragement can be of help in some way to an aspiring author, or anyone else pursuing his or her dreams, I'll continue to offer it.

A professor can never better distinguish himself in his work than by encouraging a clever pupil, for the true discoverers are among them, as comets amongst the stars.

—LINNAEUS

A friend put me in touch with Myrna because she thought that I, a self-professed positive thinker, might be able to help her. Myrna was a confirmed negative thinker and blamer and she relished that status. According to Myrna, her life had been totally miserable for as long as she could remember, and she remembered and replayed each agonizing moment, frame by frame, daily. Her parents abused her, the kids in elementary and high school teased and taunted her, her peers in college refused to socialize with her, her coworkers were mean, and her various bosses unappreciative. She never managed to complete her education, or keep a job for more than a few weeks. Her parents disowned her, her husbands left her, her children turned their backs on her, her neighbors shunned her, and her landlords constantly threatened eviction. Surrounded by all this misery and negativity, she stopped looking for employment or friends, became a ward of the state, and, finally, a virtual recluse.

> *There is a basic law that like attracts like. Negative thinking definitely attracts negative results. Conversely, if a person habitually thinks optimistically and hopefully, his positive thinking sets in motion positive forces—and success instead of eluding him flows toward him.*
>
> —NORMAN VINCENT PEALE

Obviously, Myrna was a very troubled young woman. I say young, because she was about forty, quite young by my standards. In our conversations, it became immediately apparent that she had a permanent attachment to her tragic lifestyle and did not want to change. Not receiving the pity from me that she thought she deserved, she replayed all of the hurts over and over in hopes of eliciting the sympathetic response she so desired. As time went by, her oft-told stories became more tragic and pathetic with every telling; it was almost a game of "I dare you or anyone to top my miserable life story!"

> *To be wronged is nothing unless you choose to remember it.*
>
> —CONFUCIUS

To the friend who introduced us, and to Myrna herself, I emphasized that I was not a therapist, and although I was willing to try to help, Myrna should really consult a professional. It turned out that she was actually seeing two state-provided therapists, but preferred talking to me.

I spent a great deal of time and energy and many months working with her. She refused to accept the fact that she was an adult, that she, and no one else, controlled the thoughts in her mind, or that she was, in any way, responsible for the things that kept happening to her. The resistance to change that she put up was monumental; she was determined to stay stuck in the mire of her misery and was stubbornly uninterested in the suggestions that I or her therapists offered. Positive thinking? Accept personal responsibility, even a little bit? No way! The situation was a constant drain on my emotions as day by day she became more dependent on me.

Because I refused to be shocked and angry at "them,"

the evil perpetrators in her stories, and their reputed vile actions, the remembered tales became more colorful and melodramatic with each repetition. She had long since lost credibility with me, and I was reminded of the tale of the boy who cried wolf. As Myrna's stories became more bizarre, and new ones were revealed, I waited for the *coup de grâce*, her master "no one can top this" stroke. It was soon to come.

The world is quickly bored by the recital of misfortune, and willingly avoids the sight of distress.

—W. SOMERSET MAUGHAM

Myrna announced that she wanted to move in with me so that we would have more time to discuss her problems. When I told her that was out of the question, she asked what I would do when she arrived at my doorstep with all of her worldly possessions. I told her that I would have to take her back to her home because I could not allow her to live with me, that I had my own life to lead, with my own particular set of problems and challenges, and could not devote full time to her. Furious, she turned on me, screaming, "You're just like all the others. You don't care." And then she delivered the *coup* I had been anticipating: "I'm dying . . . I have just a few months to live and you're turning me away." That was some time ago, and according to the woman who brought Myrna into my life, she continues to be hale, hearty, and healthy as a horse.

A postscript to this story: Myrna's therapists placed her in a new discussion group consisting of women her age with similar problems. Being able to talk with peers who seemed to understand the demons in her life was extremely therapeutic for Myrna. In addition, her doctors adjusted the medications she was taking to achieve the right balance. The result, after a few weeks, was remarkable. I am happy to report that while Myrna may never be free of medical supervision, she now has the tools necessary to lead a happy, fulfilling life.

> *However mean your life is, meet it and live it; do not shun it and call it bad names. It is not so bad as you are. The fault finder will find fault even in paradise. Love your life.*

> —HENRY DAVID THOREAU

A hero's story

Captain Gerald Coffee, a prisoner of war for seven years in Vietnam's famed Hanoi Hilton, is a member of the National Speakers Association, as I am. I was privileged to hear him speak at one of our local meetings some years ago. That memory was revived recently when I received an audiocassette from the association featuring Coffee's thoughts on adversity, pain, faith, challenge, and responsibility. Coffee has documented his experience in his riveting autobiography, *Beyond Survival*.

Jerry Coffee emphasizes that he is a very ordinary person, just like the rest of us. He draws from the same sources of strength that we all do. He feels strongly that many of us can overcome our own personal tragedies, professional and business setbacks, and challenges, and not just survive them, but that we can go beyond surviving them to emerge from them better and tougher than then we might have been, just as he did from his adversity. He reminds us that we all share adversities, but that he had the time and opportunity during some intense solitude to make some sense of it, to find some purpose from his adversity. Likewise, if we can find the purpose in our own personal adversity, it makes that adversity so much more bearable and meaningful, and positive as well.

Adversity is the first path to truth.

—LORD BYRON

Coffee's basic message is that we must find the purpose in our adversity; then we'll find that we are so much tougher than we think we are, physically, mentally, and emotionally. Coffee thought that when he was finally released from prison, he was home free, but not so. He was shot down in other ways several times since then, as we all are from time to time. And, he says, in our lifetimes, we all find ourselves in various prisons; sometimes they are physical, like Coffee's, sometimes they're existential—a result of financial situations, relationships, or other circumstances. But with faith in ourselves and each other, especially those closest to us, those prison doors are, more often than not, wide open. And we simply need, through faith, to find our way out.

That which does not kill me makes me stronger.

—FRIEDRICH NIETZSCHE

Coffee realizes that there are aspects of his story that could appear maudlin and meant to elicit pity, but that's not his purpose in telling his story. The message is that there is so much to be learned from adversity and challenge and pain. Of course nobody wants to volunteer for suffering; no one wishes for adversity to come into their lives, much less adversity of such magnitude as Coffee experienced. But, he stresses, we're all vulnerable; there are peaks and valleys in everyone's life, so it's important to take advantage of the valleys just as much as we find joy in the peaks; both are important for finding significance in our lives.

Coffee emphasizes the necessity of establishing and keeping credibility. He says it's important that those who have had experiences such as his, whether we wanted them or not, to recognize their inherent value and use the credibility that comes with this recognition in a positive manner to help others. If he didn't try to help people derive insight, to help them change their ideas and feelings about themselves and their relationships and capabilities, Coffee says he'd be blowing a very strong responsibility.

> *If you are distressed by anything external, the pain is not due to the thing itself, but to your own estimate of it; and you have the power to revoke it at any moment.*
>
> —MARCUS AURELIUS

If we are adults, mature adults, we must learn to take full responsibility for our lives. But what about those who are too young, or in other ways unable to take responsibility for their lives; those who have no one available or able, for a variety of reasons, to assume that responsibility for them?

Giving a helping hand to the young and underprivileged

My friend John was extremely concerned about young people who, for reasons over which they have no control, face lives of insecurity and desperation. For a number of years, he was treasurer of an organization that assisted the underprivileged. As the organization grew in size, the problems grew as well. Donations and other monies outside of John's control were squandered, the executive director was incompetent and did not live up to his responsibilities, and John was faced with serious questions about the man's honesty and integrity. Rather than become involved in what was bound to be a nasty scandal, John decided to resign. The organization basically fell apart, and funding for the youth program was terminated. There was great concern that many young people would be lost to drugs and drop out of school because their support system was gone.

John was haunted by the memory of Armon, a young boy of about twelve. He was smart as a whip, according to John, and had great potential. But he lived in the ghetto, had no role models, and only saw the seamy side of life. Shootings in his neighborhood were a regular occurrence. His mother, a caring woman, was doing the best she could, but she had other offspring to care for; the future for Armon was bleak.

John realized that he could not save all the kids who previously relied on the youth program, but he felt if he could set one of them on the right path, it might be an inspiration for others. In addition, a small-scale project could experiment with new ideas; what worked might allow a later, larger project to succeed.

So Armon became John's personal project. John saw to it that he and his mother applied to a local private Catholic school, and with the help of the administrative director there, Armon was accepted. It was determined that this multicultural, ethnically diversified school, where 30 percent of the students are on scholarship, would be an ideal place for Armon to develop his academic and social skills, and broaden his horizons.

> *There is always one moment in childhood when the door opens and lets the future in.*
>
> —GRAHAM GREENE

Obviously, John had to raise funds to pay for the annual $10,000 tuition. He set up a School Minority Scholarship Fund, sponsored car washes, bake sales, all the usual stuff, and sent out letters to members of his church requesting tax-deductible donations. Contributions dribbled in, and continue to do so, but not enough. John will probably pick up the slack, as he's committed to seeing Armon through high school.

But there were many contributions other than money; generous parties donated a computer, a printer, and software, and demonstrated how to use the equipment; a woman donated a study desk and encyclopedia set; someone else donated a study light; a nun committed to funding bus passes for Armon for the entire year; a friend sees that he has a bag lunch every day; a tenth-grader offered to tutor Armon every week; and the head-master of the school has assured John that he will personally supervise Armon so that he will always feel welcome and be able to make a smooth transition to his new life.

> *And now abideth faith, hope and charity, these*
> *three; but the greatest of these is charity.*
>   —CORINTHIANS 13:13

Recently, John sent out a progress report to those who contributed on Armon's behalf. It outlined what was working and what was not working. On the "working side," John reported:

Armon likes the school, and the school likes Armon.

Logistical things are in place: bus pass, books, com-puter, tutors, food.

Armon can do the work and is adapting to a new world.

He is overcoming his shyness and is starting to par-ticipate in class.

On the "not working" side, John made these observa-tions:

Armon must exhibit a more positive attitude in class.

He must put forth a more consistent effort.

He must do his homework and assigned projects on time.

He must participate, help others, and assist in class learning.

He must take initiative for his own learning.

He must seek out help when needed.

He and his mother must see that he has a good breakfast prior to arriving at school.

A contract covering these points was written, and signed by all concerned. John concluded the contract by saying: "We are off to a good start; could have been better, but we're all learning. Keep up the good work; Armon is worth it!" Although John and his group did not require it, it occurred to me that it could have been helpful if they had also required Armon himself to sign a contract outlining the plans for his future, thereby bringing home the meaning of "personal responsibility."

I don't know about you, but I think Armon is one lucky guy to have John and his team on his side. But the main reason I chose to include this story is to get you thinking about what you can do to help others who are too young or otherwise unable to help themselves. Think about it, and if you're moved to do so, take the initiative and responsibility today to help someone less fortunate. As Albert Camus said, "Don't wait for the Last Judgment. It takes place every day."

Our responsibilities to our pets

We all have many responsibilities in our lives; often these responsibilities include those totally unable to take on personal responsibility. I am referring to our four-legged friends: our dogs, cats, other pets, and even our farm animals.

I totally agree with George Eliot, who said, "Animals are such agreeable friends—they ask no questions, they pass no criticisms." I live with two dear four-legged friends, my dog, Charlie, and cat, PK, and I'm visited daily—sometimes hourly—by a group of neighborhood cats who belong to Hans's Breakfast Club.

The "Breakfast Club," known by all our neighbors on Clarendon Crescent, consists of five cats: Tod, Milo, Purr, Noches, and Chirpy. They have breakfast on my front porch daily. Tod, Milo, and Purr were adopted from an animal shelter by a family on another street, but these three cats haven't been to that home for several years, preferring to live on Clarendon Crescent. Noches lives down the street with Mary, who readopted Tod— at least he wears a tag with Mary's address and phone number; Milo lives up the street with a family who re-adopted and tagged him. I don't know about Chirpy's permanent home, but Purr has taken up residence in my backyard. In addition to breakfasting on the porch, all appear at my door or window several times daily to eat and visit.

Hans and I have taken on responsibility for these de-lightful cats. If we are away or unavailable for any rea-son, Mary and her daughter come to our front porch and feed breakfast to each cat in his or her individual dish on his or her individual eating spot. All of our neighbors are animal lovers, so you can understand the upset that occurred on our street after the following incident.

An unnecessary tragedy

Early one morning, the neighbors were venturing out to the curb to pick up their morning papers when suddenly the usual peace and quiet of our street was shattered by screeching brakes, a loud thump, and a piercing cry, followed by the sound of kids screaming. A beautiful young dog had been hit and killed directly in front of my house.

I had had one of my usual wide-awake nights, and finally fell into a deep sleep at dawn, so fortunately and thank God, I missed the incident and its aftermath; otherwise I would have gone to pieces. When I arose, Hans asked if I had heard anything unusual. Fearing the worst, I immediately asked, "What happened?" He started to tell me, but when I realized it concerned an animal, I couldn't bear to hear the story. I clapped my hands to my ears, to shut out his words, to my eyes, as if to cancel the picture that instantly flashed into my mind, and to my mouth, to stop my involuntary screaming of "No! No! Please, God, no!"

> *There is sorrow enough in the natural way*
> *From men and women to fill our day;*
> *But when we are certain of sorrow in store,*
> *Why do we always arrange for more?*
> *Brothers and sisters, I bid you beware*
> *Of giving your heart to a dog to tear.*

> —RUDYARD KIPLING

We were both extremely shaken by this unnecessary tragedy and determined one of us should write the Let-

ters to the Editor column of our local paper. Here is
Hans's letter:

Editor:

*The other morning the quietness of our street
was shattered by a large screeching sound followed by kids screaming. First I thought that a
child had been hit by a car, but when I looked out
of the window, I saw a beautiful black dog lying
on the pavement.*

*It appears that two young boys were riding
their bicycles down the street and their dog was
running alongside. Our street is very narrow, and
when cars are parked on both sides, there is hardly enough room for an automobile to pass. The
dog, a black Lab, was apparently running around
a parked car when he was hit by a station wagon
heading the other way. Although the driver of the
station wagon desperately tried to stop, he never
had a chance of avoiding the dog.*

*One of the kids went to fetch his mother while the
other stayed behind. Helpful and concerned neighbors rushed to see if they could assist, and possibly
take the dog to the vet. But it was too late. The
mother arrived and began sobbing uncontrollably
when she saw her beautiful young animal lying
there dead, his life snuffed out in an instant.*

*All of this could have been avoided. We do have
a dog-leash law in our city. The leash law not only
protects others from dogs, but also protects and
safeguards dogs from moving vehicles. Unfortunately, many people do not obey the leash law,
hence these tragedies.*

It is not a pretty sight when an animal is run over by a vehicle, not to mention what it does emotionally to those that are in some way involved. The poor driver of the station wagon that killed the black Lab was totally distraught. He pulled his car over to the curb and sat on his front bumper with his head in his hands for over an hour. I am sure the owners of the dog, in retrospect, wish they had the chance to start that day over differently.

The lesson to be learned is: Be responsible. If you love your dog and value its life, please keep it on a leash and under control at all times. Or, allow it to run in an area designated for such a purpose.

I invite your comments.

A day or so later Hans received this e-mail from Ann:

You wrote a great letter in the 12/4/98 Montclarion. I couldn't agree with you more. I would feel extremely sad if I hit an animal running loose, and although I would feel sorry for the owner, I just think it's plain stupidity. People should take responsibility for their animals. I think I would sue the owner for my own emotional strain at having killed an animal.

I have a neighbor who lets her animals run loose and I don't know what is the matter with these people. My dog is a cherished member of my family.

I was relating this story to Amelia, my veterinarian friend, when she interrupted and said, "Alice, you don't have to tell me; I see this constantly in my practice. And it's totally unnecessary. People are so irresponsible. If they want to have pets, they should be forced to take responsibility for them!"

After we talked about responsibility for one's pets for a bit, she again interrupted me. "Boy, you've hit one of my hot buttons with this responsibility issue! I could write a book—make that a couple of books—on the matter. And I'd start at the very beginning. People should analyze why they want a dog or cat. Do they want a companion, a family member—or a toy for the kids?" And because this was shortly before Christmas, Amelia went on to say that she, and all vets, caution against getting an animal as a holiday gift for a young child. "Christmas is just the wrong time to get a new pet. There's too much going on, too much confusion, too many distractions, and not enough time to spend with the pet in order to integrate it into the household."

"In many ways," Amelia went on, "pets are like little children. They're curious, they put everything in their mouths, and they don't take no for an answer. People must remember that in many ways, a dog or cat is like a perpetual toddler; they really need a lot of supervision, especially when they're puppies or kittens.

"Another thing that's important, and this is a big issue with me," continued Amelia, "is that people don't give enough consideration to the type of dog, its breed, size, and temperament, when choosing one. They forget that they're making a choice for the lifetime of the animal. They see a cute puppy at the shop or shelter, and don't consider what he'll be like when he's fully grown and mature."

I agreed with Amelia wholeheartedly. Charlie came

to me because his original owners, thinking him cute and adorable as a teeny puppy, quickly tired of his yapping and jumping, which is simply the nature of the spitz or, as the American Kennel Club labels him, American Eskimo dog. He had been sent off to an animal shelter and possible euthanasia when a friend rescued him for me without even asking if I'd take him. We had recently lost our adorable Calorie, and were still grieving for her. I didn't feel I was quite ready for a new dog, but told the friend that I'd see that Charlie got a good home. Yes, I certainly did!

In another instance, some friends of Hans's bought a full-bred registered cocker spaniel as a surprise Christmas gift for their very young daughter. Princess was a novelty for a while—a short while—until the mother realized she was not yet housebroken. No one wanted to take the time or responsibility of training the dog, so Princess was relegated to the garage and totally ignored by the family, including the little girl who had quickly tired of her new "toy."

After a year or so, because they knew we were animal lovers, the family asked us to find Princess a new home, which we were able to do through the agency that had found us our beloved Calorie. But just think of poor Princess, alone in a dark garage for over a year! Naturally, she was still not trained when her new owner adopted her, but I'm sure with all the love that woman had to offer, Princess was able to catch on quickly.

The greatest pleasure of a dog is that you may make a fool of yourself with him and not only will he not scold you, but he will make a fool of himself as well.

—SAMUEL BUTLER

Being financially and legally responsible

We've touched on some aspects of the enormous subject of responsibility and its corollary, trustworthiness; there are many more. The need for responsibility also makes itself abundantly apparent in the area of finances, and in the vast legal field as well.

Obviously, if we are responsible people, and trustworthy, we pay our bills, our debts, our taxes, and our alimony, if the latter pertains to us, and we make sure that our checks do not bounce. We support ourselves and our families and educate our children to the best of our abilities. We do not spend beyond our means, and we don't abuse our credit. We invest wisely and do not take unnecessary risks. And in preparation for our eventual demise, we make sure our affairs are in order. We are financially responsible.

And if we are responsible people, and trustworthy, we see that we live up to our legal contracts and obey all laws, including those of the land and the road. We are legally responsible.

But if we were all responsible people, would we need the plethora of lawyers that abounds in this country? Would we have the number of lawsuits that glut our courts? Would we need the number of courts and judges that are required to handle them? Good questions to ponder.

Let us reread the definitions of responsibility and apply them to our lives. Let us take responsibility, either blame or credit, for our conduct and obligations. Let us be trustworthy. Let us be mature adults, willing and able to discharge difficult or exacting duties, to delegate wisely, and to perform capably despite unforeseen obstacles. Let us be accepters, not blamers; actors, not reactors.

Let us be responsible; let us be trustworthy. John Powell, S.J., an author of many books and professor at Loyola University in Chicago, suggests putting this sign on your bathroom mirror:

You are looking at the face of the person who is responsible for your happiness.

Yes, you, and only you, are responsible for your happiness. Start today to take responsibility—full personal responsibility—for your life, and prepare for the happiness that is sure to follow.

My Resolutions

In regard to Commandment IV, *Be Responsible and Trustworthy in All Ways,* these are my resolutions:

....

....

....

....

....

....

....

....

....

....

....

....

....

....

....

....

....

....

....

....

....

....

Honor Your Relationships

*No man is an island, entire of itself;
every man is a piece of the continent,
a part of the main. Any man's death
diminishes me, because I am involved in mankind; and therefore
never send to know for whom the bell
tolls; it tolls for thee.*

—JOHN DONNE

HOW true! We cannot live an isolated existence.
Like it or not, we are all constantly involved with
other people, we all have, and have had, relationships of
one kind or another since the day we were born. And
we will continue to have relationships for the rest of our
lives because, as Donne says, "No man is an island."

Parents and the family—our primary relationship

Our first, and perhaps most influential relationship, is
with our parents and immediate family. My earliest
memories revolve around my dad, who was my hero,
my mother, who was the disciplinarian, and a strict one,

according to my youthful perception, and my little sister, who was delivered by the stork when I was about six.

I must have had an idyllic childhood, although I didn't have the sense to realize it at the time, or even much later. I was brought up in a small suburban town with tree-lined streets and friendly neighbors who knew just about every family in the immediate area and everything that was going on in those families' lives, or so it seemed.

> *It is easier to love humanity as a whole than to love one's neighbors.*
>
>   —ERIC HOFFER

I expect that ours was a typical upper-middle-class family. Dad, a banker, went daily to The Bank, the only way we ever referred to his place of employment. Mother was a full-time homemaker, of course. Early on, I was appointed mother's helper, albeit reluctantly, in the area of household chores and kitchen duties, and while it was obviously good training for me, I cannot say I relished the role. My best friend was Gloria, and her family had a maid who tended to those boring details, so I felt put-upon to be saddled with such mundane tasks. When we're young, and have little with which to compare, we often have no idea how fortunate we are.

As with most families, we had our rituals. Nightly, and twice on Sunday when we had dinner at noon and supper in the evening, we sat around the dining-room table that Alice set and cleared. During the meal, Dad expounded at length on the happenings and politics of the day, the state of the Union and the neighborhood,

and other things that irritated him. The three of us—
Mother, Ann, and I—were a captive audience. No one
dared to express an opinion; in fact, we had no opinions;
girls and women simply didn't in those days.

After dessert, and we always had dessert, a custom I
gave up years ago, Dad and I attended to our assigned
duties of dish dryer and dishwasher respectively, I trying
to coax a semblance of suds out of uncooperative slivers
of leftover soap—no grease-emulsifying detergents in
those days—and hard water, while Dad dried as he
puffed away on his evil-smelling after-dinner stogie,
nearly asphyxiating us all in the process.

Weekday evenings we listened to *Easy Aces* followed
by Lowell Thomas and the news; on Sunday it was *The
Jack Benny Show* followed by *The Chase and Sandborn
Hour*, featuring Edgar Bergen and Charlie McCarthy.
There was no television, of course, and no one ever considered turning on the radio during the day or at any
time without Dad's permission. The radio was Dad's
private domain and only he controlled the knobs. If there
was something earth-shattering to be heard when Dad
was at The Bank, Mother would call him for permission
and instructions in regard to properly turning on and
tuning in of the radio.

I said that Mother was a strict disciplinarian, and she
was. Just let me be five minutes late coming home from
Gloria's house and there was hell to pay. My excuse
was that I didn't have a watch; Mother did not accept
excuses. The instant I realized I was in for it, I raced to
the stairs with Mother, all four feet eleven inches,
ninety-eight pounds of her, armed with whatever spanking instrument she could put her hands on, hot on my
tail.

He that spareth the rod hateth his son: but he that loveth him chasteneth him betimes.

—PROVERBS 13:24

At the top of the stairs I sprinted for the nearest room, usually the bedroom I shared with Ann, and locked myself in. Mother would pound on the door with her spanking instrument, threatening the most dire of consequences if I didn't come out instantly. I was not about to budge, crying, "I want my dad-dy!" Throughout the day, as the threats and proposed dire consequences escalated, my cry remained the same, "I want my dad-dy!"

Dad always came to the rescue, patiently explaining to Mother that if concessions were not made, with the problem solved by talking rather than spanking, Alice would never come out. Grimly, Mother would finally agree, and I would timidly open the door, allowing life to continue, temporarily.

After several such flights, I realized that there was a definite disadvantage to holing up in the bedroom; despite it being a haven, there was no plumbing. Henceforth, I barricaded myself in the bathroom, where there was the luxury of running water and a toilet. It, too, was a safe haven, but its disadvantage was that there was no reading material; I became bored waiting for Dad to rescue me. I solved that problem by hiding funny books and what were called "Big Little Books" in the back of the pedestal sink where the plumbing fixtures are located. Since we never had need for a plumber, no one ever found my stash of reading material. But Mother soon tired of our "fight and flight" episodes and had the locks removed from all of the upstairs rooms, including the bathroom. When I went back to the old homestead for a visit many years later, the locks were still absent, everyone in the family claiming to have no knowledge as to why they were ever removed.

> *Children begin by loving their parents. After a time they judge them. Rarely, if ever, do they forgive them.*
>
> —OSCAR WILDE

They say if you ever want to be treated like a child again, go home and visit your parents. How true that is! Every time I went back home, even as a full-fledged adult, a married woman with children, and later as a single working parent, I was instantly relegated, once again, to the tender age of twelve. One afternoon, during the winter, with its short days, I was visiting old school friends and returned to my parents home slightly after dark. Just like in the old days, it was, "Do you realize what time it is? It's five-thirty! You have no business being out after dark all alone. Don't let it happen again!"

I thought their protectiveness extended only to the old home territory, not my out-of-state residence. But no, I found out that when we were together, it continued to apply everywhere and anywhere. Mother and Dad were visiting me in my home in upstate New York; I was in my thirties at the time, had a full-time job, and was buying my first home. In other words, I was a responsible adult.

I invited my parents to the officers' club for dinner, where, even though I was a military widow, I still had dining privileges. My son, Mark, who was about ten or eleven, accompanied us. Because it was Saturday night, there was a band at the club; couples were dancing. I alternately danced with Mark and Dad. An officer sitting at an adjoining table watched us with amusement. Dad invited him to join us and soon I was dancing with the officer, and Mother was dancing with Dad, who was secretly gloating over his role as Cupid. Mark was glad to simply observe.

After dinner, Dad invited the officer to accompany us back to my house for coffee, which he did. Dad and Mother soon exited, saying they were tired after a long day. The officer and I continued to sit in my den drinking coffee and talking. Suddenly Dad appeared at the top of the stairs to the den in his pajamas and robe. "Young man, do you know what time it is? It's after eleven, not a decent time for you and my daughter to be alone. Please leave!" Of course, the officer left. I was mortified. Later, I was highly amused, but at the time, I was a bit miffed with Dad.

> *Crabbed youth and age cannot live together;*
> *Youth is full of pleasure, age is full of care.*
>
> —WILLIAM SHAKESPEARE

Yes, parents can be hard to understand sometimes, but at least in my case, their often smothering concern and overprotectiveness *was* understandable; after all, they were *parents*! If you have children of your own, you can appreciate this. Naturally, I determined that I'd be an entirely different kind of mother: a friend, buddy, and confidante to my children. That didn't have the desired effect either, it seems, at least not in the case of my daughter, who enjoys telling all within earshot about how badly I fell down on the job. I think she wanted a stay-at-home mother who baked bread, cakes, and cookies all day. I did just that, but on my TV cooking show, *For You Madame*. It was a given that I had to work, but I think she would have preferred me to have a mundane office job rather than one that put me in the spotlight.

> *How sharper than a serpent's tooth it is to have a thankless child!*
>
> —WILLIAM SHAKESPEARE

If you are fortunate enough to have parents who are still living, please, *please,* let them know that you appreciate them and all they did for you. Even if your childhood memories are less than perfect, or even hardly pleasant, there must be something nice you can say to the two people who gave you life and took care of you in your early years. If you are a parent yourself, you can certainly understand the frustrations that little ones can unknowingly cause; in your present state of maturity, isn't it time you gave your parents a break? They may have been too young and naive when you were born to know any better, and really did the best that they could under what may have been trying circumstances. As the saying goes, "Babies do not come with a how-to manual."

Say thank you

To express your love and appreciation, some suggest you simply say, "I love you," or "I appreciate all you

did for me when I was a kid." You can do this in person
or on the phone. If speaking out like that seems intimidating to you, put it in writing. If you can't find the
right words, head toward your local card shop. Hallmark
and others are specialists in this type of thing.

>   *Honor thy father and thy mother.*
>   —EXODUS 20:12

Years ago, after Mother died and Dad was alone, I became nostalgic remembering these two important people
in my life, and wrote Dad a letter thanking him for some
of the things that came to mind. After receiving it, all
he said to me was, "I got your letter. Thank you." He
didn't have to say more. After his death, I came across
the letter in his things. Although he had lots of business
and financial correspondence, my letter was the only
piece of personal mail he had saved.

When he was dying, Dad called me in California one
morning and asked, "How soon can you get out here? I
want to see you." I took an afternoon flight and arrived
in New Jersey close to midnight. When I appeared in
his living room, he and his caretaker, Mazie, applauded
wildly. "Turn around; I want to *really* see you," Dad
commanded. I did a pirouette and curtsied, to more
applause. To Mazie, Dad said, "This is my little girl."
Instantly, I understood his years of concern and overprotectiveness. I was his little girl, and always would be.
And he was my father, my daddy, and always would be.

I stayed only a few days, to my everlasting regret.
On one of those nights, I tucked Dad in bed and leaned

over to kiss him good night. I looked into his eyes, which were still a beautiful blue, and noticed something I'd not seen before. "Dad," I exclaimed, "you have a twinkle!" And he did; he had a marvelous, mischievous twinkle. Dad laughed out loud, uproariously, as if we were sharing a wonderful joke. I'll never forget that experience. Please, look for the twinkle in the eyes of an important person in your life. Don't let him or her go before you find it. You will be forever glad that you did.

Friends and the school experience

As we grow, our horizons expand and we begin to foster relationships outside of the family unit. First, there are the kids and families in the immediate neighborhood, which, depending on our age, gradually expands. Then we enter school and a whole new world of relationships with other children, some from areas outside of our own, children we may not like or understand. In addition, instead of our known authority figures, we encounter an entirely different set: teachers, principals, advisers, and counselors.

> *The little world of childhood with its familiar surroundings is a model of the greater world. The more intensively the family has stamped its character upon the child, the more it will tend to feel and see its earlier miniature world again in the bigger world of adult life.*
>
> —CARL JUNG

My school years were relatively happy and free from care. But that is not the case with many. My sister, who obviously came from the same family background as I, and went through the same school system, says she didn't enjoy her school years. She seems reluctant to explain why. She is not alone; many refuse to attend their high-school reunions saying simply that they're "overwhelming glad to have gotten away from all of those people." On the other hand, I think going to a reunion of my alma mater, Millburn High School, ranks high in the category of fun and excitement. And when I do attend a reunion, as I did recently, the conversation always gets around to how fortunate we all were to have had the privilege and opportunity of attending such wonderful schools where we actually learned what we were supposed to.

> *Education is what survives when what has been learnt has been forgotten.*
>
> —B. F. SKINNER

When I remember those days, the thing that comes to mind most is the friendships I made, friendships that have endured lo these many years. To this day, I can name all of the kids on my street, and probably the names of their dogs as well. My close personal friends from school, the ones I see at reunions, are very special to me. It's amazing, I thought to myself at the last one: here we are a bunch of senior citizens, standing around laughing and talking just as we did back in the old days. It was as if time stood still. I pondered the gray or lost hair, glasses, expanded waistlines, and other physical changes. How did that happen? Obviously, we were all still teenagers at heart. Where did the years go?

*The more the pleasures of the body fade away,
the greater to me is the pleasure and charm of
conversation.*

—PLATO

Nurture those school and childhood relationships, they
are very special. Even without reunions, I continue to
correspond with those in my class, mostly at Christmas,
and now, with the advent of e-mail, letters from schoolmates are liable to arrive at any time.

New people can become friends

You may feel that schoolmates are like relatives; that
we had no choice in the matter. The Cynic's Calendar
states, "God gives us our relatives—thank God we can
choose our friends." How very true, especially for those
of you who have less than pleasant memories concerning
schoolmates and relatives. But how does one choose a
friend? How does one become a friend? I honestly don't
know, it just seems to happen.

Speaking as the world's shyest child and teenager, I
can tell you with all honesty that making new friends
can be a most intimidating experience. Everyone else
seems cool and collected, in total control of themselves
and all situations, and here you are, a quivering mass of
insecurity, scared to death to say anything for fear of
being laughed at, always hanging around the outskirts
of the fun, wishing you had the magic ingredient that
would produce instant acceptability.

That's when you need to know that as James Russell
Lowell said, "Whatever you may be sure of, be sure of

this—that you are dreadfully like other people." Yes, we are all dreadfully like other people. Regardless of our age or status, we all desire to be important and to feel appreciated. And this starts in our very earliest years. If you finally "get" this, it can help you tremendously, not only in acquiring friends, but in every single aspect of your personal life and in all of your various relationships.

It was about this time of my life, the shy preadolescent years, that I purchased by first self-help book, *How to Win Friends and Influence People* by Dale Carnegie. As I recall, it cost me three weeks' allowance, and I never mentioned its possession to anyone. I didn't want to be laughed at for buying such a book, or for feeling that I couldn't figure the whole thing out by myself, as everyone else seemed to do. Of all the things I ever read or was exposed to in my early years, this book, by Carnegie, probably had the single greatest impact on my thinking and approach to other people. It offers six ways of making people like you; they are as relevant today as they were when he wrote the book over sixty years ago. Because these rules made such an impression on me, I'll list them here for you:

- Become genuinely interested in other people.

- Smile.

- Remember that a man's name to him is the sweetest and most important sound in any language.

- Be a good listener. Encourage others to talk about themselves.

- Talk in terms of the other man's interest.

- Make the other person feel important—and do it sincerely.

I am not alone in praising Carnegie; within the last couple of months, I've had others in diverse circumstances bring up the book and express the same view: that this was an important book in establishing their personal approach to, and acceptance of, other people.

William James said, "The deepest principle of human nature is the craving to be appreciated." If you can help other people feel important and appreciated, they are going to like you, they will desire your company, they will want you to be their friend. In other words, put their interests ahead of yours. Search for their good points so you can truthfully appreciate and praise them. The key word here is "truthfully." No one likes a "yes-man" or apple-polisher, a phony. People can see through glib praise. You must search for the qualities that you truly admire so that you can praise and appreciate these characteristics with full honesty.

A true friend is the most precious of all possessions and the one we take the least thought about acquiring.

—LA ROCHEFOUCAULD

A moment ago I asked the questions: How does one choose a friend and how does one become a friend? The better question might be: How does one *remain* a friend? Some of the things that come to my mind include:

- Be there for your friend when he or she needs you.

- Listen. *Really* listen.

- Only give advice when asked, and then be exceedingly tactful.

- Criticize *carefully,* with love and understanding, and only if absolutely necessary.

- Be tolerant, not judgmental.

- Show appreciation.

- Be kind.

- Believe in your friend.

- Offer and give support where and when needed, and do not expect anything in return.

- Keep your promises.

- Continually thank your friend for all favors, small as well as large.

- Do not gossip about your friend.

- Forgive as you would be forgiven.

- And, last of all, be yourself.

Samuel Johnson said, "If a man does not make new acquaintances as he advances through life, he will soon find himself left alone." Hope, then, that some of the new acquaintances you make will become friends, and work toward that end by applying the above list of attributes. Actually, I think the list is a good one to apply to *all* relationships.

Neighborly relations

How well do you get along with your neighbors? Personally, I can't think of a worse scenario than the Hatfield vs. McCoy kind of relationship, and I will go to all lengths to avoid conflict. Hans, on the other hand, is ready to go to battle over the slightest thing.

Our wonderful, congenial neighbors, Roger and Vicki, had just gotten a new dog, Scruffy. Of undetermined origin, Scruffy fits his name to a tee and as most dogs, he has an insatiable appetite. The problem is that he discovered where to find an unlimited supply of food to feed that appetite: on our front porch, where Hans puts out goodies several times a day for his Breakfast Club.

Hans would put out five dishes of food, one for each cat in the club, plus a community bowl or two of nuggets. Five minutes later, after Scruffy's intervention, before the cats had a chance to nosh, every morsel would be devoured, the plates licked sparkling clean, sometimes even the plates would be missing. After several such instances, Hans had had his fill of the intruder. "That damn dog! How dare he eat all my cat food every time I put it out!"

"Come on, Hans, calm down. He's only a dog, and a lovable one at that," I'd say. "Oh yeah?" would be Hans's retort. "What's he doing over here anyway? Don't they know about the leash law?" As you know from his letter to the editor, the leash law is a big thing with Hans. "Do they have any idea how much I spend on this cat food? I'm going next door and give them a piece of my mind!" "Hans! They are our neighbors, and very good ones. Cool it. I'm sure Charlie and his barking bothers them at times, too. Just knock it off." And so it went for a time. I felt as if I were sitting on a powder keg.

Then one day the doorbell rang, and when I answered, there was a gift bag sitting on the front doormat with a note sticking out. The note was written on a card picturing a cat that was the image of Tod, the charter member of the Breakfast Club, and Hans's favorite. It said:

> *Dear Hans and Alice.*
>   *Sorry to keep eating Tod's cat food and stealing the bowls.*
>   *I don't think I can steal this one.*
>   *My mom and dad send this wine with their apologies and hope you enjoy it.*
>   *Your unruly neighbor,*
>   *Scruffy*

Inside the bag was a large, sturdy ceramic bowl suitable for cat food or nuggets; too heavy for easy transportation by mouth, and two bottles of wine. Now, that is what I call a neighborly thing to do!

But that is part one of the story. As I said to Hans, perhaps Charlie bothers them on occasion. To my chagrin, it turned out that he did.

One Sunday morning when I went out front to pick up the newspaper, I noticed a letter attached to the mailbox. It was addressed to "Hans & Alice." This is what it said:

> *Dear Hans & Alice:*
> *Vicki and I respectfully request you to consider*

*not putting Charlie in your backyard prior to 7:30
A.M. (possibly eight A.M. on weekends) and after
9:30 P.M. As you may or may not realize, our bedroom is directly above your backyard. And with a
one-year-old and another baby on its way, I'm
sure you can understand sleep is a precious com-
modity around our house. When Charlie goes to
your backyard, he barks incessantly at everything
(or nothing!)—birds, noises, critters, etc. His
barking has frequently awakened us after we have
fallen asleep in the evening and while we are still
trying to sleep in the morning.*

*Your consideration on this matter would be
greatly appreciated. Thanks.*

                                             Roger

Now it was our turn to be in the hot seat! Charlie, my
baby, was disturbing the neighbors. I was aghast. Maybe
I was so accustomed to his seal-like bark that I no longer
heard it. Maybe our house is so soundproof that when
Charlie goes outside and barks, I cannot hear it inside.
But it was true; in the morning, when Charlie is released
from the house, just like a rooster he announces the new
day and his presence in it.

What to do about this problem? Years ago, when we
first got Charlie and realized that he barked a lot, someone suggested we have his vocal cords cut; a ghastly
thought. But, after receiving Roger and Vicki's note, I
called the vet anyway, just to get his thoughts on various
solutions. As far as the vocal-cords thing, the vet's advice was, "Absolutely not!" But he did suggest that we
look into battery-operated antibarking devices that are
incorporated into special dog collars. I immediately

called local pet stores and every catalog operation that offered such devices. Then, armed with a variety of solutions, I went to see Roger and Vicki to tell them of my efforts, and to ask for their patience while we attempted to put the solutions into practice.

They were very understanding, especially when they saw my concern and desire to correct the situation. We tried an antibarking collar briefly; it didn't work with Charlie. What we ended up doing was letting him out after 7:30 A.M. weekdays, and 8:30 A.M. weekends, but just seconds before he was served breakfast. He was so anxious to get inside again to instantly consume his morning meal that he panted at the door after an initial bark or two. Then he was content to stay in the house until a reasonable hour, when he was again let out briefly. For some reason, he never barked when let out the second time; his early barking was simply a "here I am, world" kind of thing. In the evening, I personally go with him in the backyard. Every time he takes a big breath that I know is going to end in a bark, I strictly warn, "No barking, Charlie." The minute he takes care of his needs, I instruct him to come back inside with me. The problem seems to be resolved.

Remember Donne's words, "No man is an island . . ." We all must interact with others, and in our densely populated cities and crowded suburban areas, we are bound to cause problems for those close by, or irritate them, albeit unknowingly, just as they do us. Don't make a federal case out of it. Resolve the situation by civilized means. Make a peace offering, as Roger and Vicki did. Talk it out, as I did with them. Above all, don't let the matter cause hostility and ongoing anger.

No one needs or wants that kind of tension surrounding their home environment.

Workplace relations

Career Coach Marty Nemko, in his weekly column *Under the Radar* in the Sunday *San Francisco Examiner Chronicle*, offers three magic words:

> The three truly magic words aren't "Abracadabra, hocus pocus." If I want magical conversations, whether in business or personal interactions, I look for a way to honestly say "I RESPECT you," "I APPRECIATE you" or "I AGREE with you." Those three words can sometimes, like magic, turn a discussion from adversarial to collaborative, from cordial to inspired. To remind me to use "respect," "appreciate" and "agree," there's a Post-it by my phone bearing just those words. Hotel chain founder Bill Marriott offers a variation: He says the four most important words are "What do you think?"

Good advice, Marty. Let us all heed these three magic words. And there is no place where they are more needed than in the workplace. You are stuck with relatives who did not come to you by choice, but you usually don't have to see them on a daily basis. You choose your friends, so it's assumed that you like, tolerate, and enjoy being with them. But what about those people you see day in and day out, Monday through Friday, for eight or more hours at a stretch—what about your employers, employees, and coworkers?

It is in the workplace that Marty's three magic words make the greatest difference, the difference between success and congeniality, or stress and dissatisfaction. In fact, your employment and livelihood can literally depend on your utilizing his three magic words. To them I'd like to add some words of my own: LISTEN, really listen, to your boss, employee or coworker, CONSIDER their viewpoint or solution; and be WILLING to implement the plan or follow the orders issued. This is no time to let your ego or pride interfere with what is best for the overall operation. Be a TEAM PLAYER. And, be GRATEFUL for your job, especially if it's one you like. As Thomas Carlyle said, "Blessed is he who has found his work. Let him ask no other blessedness."

When work is a pleasure, life is a joy!
When work is duty, life is slavery.

                              —MAXIM GORKY

Personal relationships

When most of us think about relationships, we think of our *personal* relationships, ones that are usually romantic in nature and often go beyond friendship, such as the *intimate* relationship we have with our spouse, lover, or significant other.

When the relationship starts, everything is rosy, the loved one can do or say no wrong. It's been said that you think you are in love, but you are really in lust! The Greek dramatist Menander said, "Love blinds all men, both the reasonable and the foolish." Then what happens? Why do almost 50 percent of marriages end in divorce? Why do committed couples break up? Reality rears its ugly head! We begin to see the loved one for who he or she really is. Those funny little habits that seemed so endearing in the beginning of the relationship can suddenly become irritating beyond measure.

What can we do to maintain a healthy, happy relationship? We can start by referring to the list of ways to remain a good friend mentioned in the previous chapter. And we can refer to Marty Nemko's three magic words and the words that I added to his. To this we can add an additional word: *honor*. Yes, honor your relationship; hold it in the highest regard.

Another important word is *communicate*. If you can openly communicate your true thoughts, feelings, and needs without fear of being put down by your partner, you can feel safe in being yourself. If you cannot safely be yourself in all ways within your relationship, it is doomed. Just as you want to be yourself, allow your partner to be himself, do not try to force him into the mold of your expectations, which, for him, may not be comfortable or realistic.

It may be said that a relationship is an investment, an investment in time, energy, and emotion, and as such, it can be the most important investment you will ever make. Therefore, be cautious before making the commitment. Once the commitment is made, put yourself into the relationship wholeheartedly, no holds barred, as you would put yourself into an important business or financial investment or commitment. Invest your time, invest your energy, invest your emotion in this all-important aspect of your life.

Set goals for your relationship just as you would do for your career or business. How do you and your partner envision your lives together during the next year, five years from now, down the road, and into the sunset? There are many things to consider, among them: where you will live, career plans, children, the responsibility of pets, leisure activities, and eventual retirement and how to spend it. Above all, heed the advice of Kahlil Gibran, who said, "Let there be spaces in your togetherness."

> *There is no more lovely, friendly, charming relationship, communion, or company than a good marriage.*
>
> **—MARTIN LUTHER**

Having pets—a win-win relationship

Your relationship with your dog, cat, bird, snake, horse, or whatever animal you have welcomed into your heart and home environment can be enriching and rewarding beyond measure. Not only that, but studies prove that pet ownership can enhance health and well-being in people of all ages.

Pets can be marvelous companions for children, especially in single-child families. Pets help teach children responsibility, social skills, as well as tolerance, sensitivity, and concern for other beings.

> *The dog was created especially for children. He is the god of frolic.*
>
> **—HENRY WARD BEECHER**

For adults, pets can help lower blood pressure, decrease the risk of heart attacks, reduce stress, and increase the ability to cope. For seniors, pets provide companionship, greater life satisfaction, and increased longevity. For those who live alone, pets counteract the damaging effects of loneliness and depression, while giving life new meaning, richness, and humor. Results are so positive that I understand one insurance company has even reduced premiums for seniors who have pets. For all of us, our pet relationships can give our lives new meaning, provide structure, and add spontaneity and laughter to our often harried days. And if you have a dog whom you walk daily, as I do Charlie, your pet can help you lose weight, tone your body, and add years to your life.

There must be a reason why the dog is known as man's best friend, and I believe it is because dogs love unconditionally. They have few of the nasty attributes common to so many humans. In her book, *Pack of Two*, Caroline Knapp points out that "Spite has no part in a dog's emotional repertoire. The same is true for hypocrisy, sarcasm, bitterness, vanity, envy and sadism. It is interesting that dogs share most of our positive emotions but few of our negative ones." Knapp notes, correctly, that dogs are almost always in a good mood. And the way dogs give love, even when it's unrequited, is nothing short of miraculous.

An animal's eyes have the power to speak a great language.

—MARTIN BUBER

When I was general manager of KRE AM and FM in Berkeley, we always had a resident dog. It gave the entire operation a warmer, far more friendly feeling and atmosphere, an opinion frequently expressed by those who visited the station, including top stars and big names in the music and recording industry. The few who seemed surprised by being greeted at the door by a four-legged wagger merely shook their heads and said, "Only in Berkeley!" As Knapp puts it, "Dogs widen rather than narrow our social world. In this ability they are like children. Wise the company that encourages its employees to bring their dogs to work."

To my surprise and delight, I recently read about the first-ever national "Take Your Dog to Work Day" sponsored by Pet Sitters International, the North Carolina company that came up with the idea. At least 250 companies took part in the day across the United States, but that only accounted for the ones who wrote in for advice on how to do it. Word is that many more participated and a great time was had by all.

If you'd like more love in your life, or if you have some extra love to give, consider getting a dog or a cat, or any other type of pet you're likely to find at a pet store. Better still, go to your local animal shelter or humane society and rescue an animal. You'll be forever glad you did.

The single most important relationship— the one you have with yourself

Throughout life, relationships come and go, they escalate, terminate, and change in nature. When you become an adult, you leave your parents' nest, just as your children will leave yours. Relatives remain relatives, but when we become adults with the freedom of choice, we can make personal decisions as to whether or not we care to continue the relationship. Your relationships with childhood friends mature; some continue, others change, as do the participants; many terminate. Friendly co-workers are often forgotten or fall by the wayside as we change jobs and locations. Other relationships come and go; affairs end, as do many marriages; divorce is accepted, often expected.

But throughout all of these changes and transitions, one relationship remains: your relationship with yourself. As the Roman playwright Terence said, "My closest relation is myself." Since that is as true as anything can be, doesn't it make sense to attempt to understand yourself, tolerate yourself, honor and acknowledge yourself, appreciate and forgive yourself, enjoy and encourage yourself, love and be kind to yourself, and, above all, forgive yourself?

> *Because I am the only person I will have a relationship with all of my life, I choose:*
>
> * *To love myself the way I am now*
> * *To always acknowledge that I am enough just the way I am*
> * *To love, honor and cherish myself*
> * *To be my own best friend*
> * *To be the person I would like to spend the rest of my life with*
> * *To always take care of myself so that I can take care of others*
> * *To always grow, develop and share my love and life.*
>
> —PETER MCWILLIAMS and JOHN ROGER,
> *You Can't Afford the Luxury of a Negative Thought*

You are unique, no one else on this planet is exactly like you; you have talents that are yours alone; you have many, many accomplishments to be proud of; your inner beauty is waiting to shine through if you will only let it; you have much to offer the world.

Applaud yourself for being who you are. Do not do this out of conceit, narcissism, or boastfulness, but rather out of pride, honest pride in your accomplishments, inner beauty, humanity, compassion, and love for your fellowman. If these words do not ring true for you, please do not delude yourself. As Plato said, "The worst of all deceptions is self-deception."

This above all: to thine own self be true,
And it must follow, as the night the day,
Thou canst not then be false to any man.

—WILLIAM SHAKESPEARE

If you want to improve yourself and your ongoing relationship with the person who will be with you until your dying day, there is much you can do. The first and most important thing is to *desire* to improve and/or change. Then you must take action. Suggested ways include reading self-help books, attending lectures, workshops, and seminars devoted to self-improvement, becoming truly aware of your thoughts, actions, and attitudes combined with taking positive, sincere steps toward changing what needs to be changed, and praying for help and guidance.

The man who masters himself is delivered from the force that binds all creatures.

—GOETHE

The ultimate relationship

There is only one other relationship, and that is the primary one. It is the relationship you had before you were born that will continue after your death and into eternity. This is the relationship you have with your Lord, Jehovah, your Heavenly Father, the Supreme Being, the Almighty, the Infinite Spirit, or whatever you choose to call God.

> *Thou shalt love the Lord thy God with all thy heart, and with all thy soul, and with all thy mind.*
>
> —MATTHEW 22:37

If you have not already done so, establish a relationship with God. God loves you for who you are. He does not care what you have done in the past; He only knows the good things you can do in the future. He does not care if you are rich or poor, what color you are, where you live, or what kind of a car you drive. He does not care about your status, bank account, or titles. He only cares about you because you are his beloved child, and He loves you. He will not desert you as others may have done in the past; He, alone, is totally faithful. He will listen to you at any time day or night; He is ready and waiting to help you with your biggest problems and smallest concerns. He simply asks that you turn to Him in your hour of need so that He can relieve your mind, relax your body, and soothe your soul.

Today, right now, might be a good time to start a relationship with your God. He is waiting to hear from you!

Ask, and it shall be given you; seek, and ye shall find; knock, and it shall be opened unto you.

—MATTHEW 7:7

Make a commitment to yourself, now, to obey Commandment V, to honor your relationships.

My Resolutions

In regard to Commandment V, *Honor Your Relationships,* these are my resolutions:

....

....

....

....

....

....

....

....

....

....

....

....

....

....

....

....

....

....

....

....

....

....

....

....

Live Up to Your Potential
and
Do Whatever It Takes

Most people live, whether physically, intellectually or morally, in a very restricted circle of their potential being. They make use of a very small portion of their possible consciousness, and of their soul's resources in general, much like a man who, out of his whole bodily organism, should get into a habit of using and moving only his little finger. Great emergencies and crises show us how much greater our vital resources are than we supposed.

—WILLIAM JAMES

IF you believe James's observation, as I do, that most people live in a very restricted circle of their potential being, the thought can be quite appalling. It bears out what many surveys have shown, that most people use only 3 percent of their abilities; the other 97 percent is basically wasted. Incredible, yet probably, and very sadly, true. And why is it that we must wait for great emergencies and crises to show us how much greater our vital resources are than we supposed? As Charles Schulz said, "Life is like a ten-speed bike. Most of us have gears we never use."

Potential, to me, is a great word. I enjoy contemplating it and its veiled meanings. Potential is closely linked to the word "potent," which means having power, strength, and influence. It implies things that exist in possibility, that are capable of developing into actuality, of greatness waiting to materialize.

I believe that we all possess vast quantities of untapped potential. *Where is it? How can we recognize it? How do we release it?* We'll search for the answers to these profound questions shortly. First, allow me to digress for a moment.

In the mid-eighties, after I retired from broadcasting and before I started writing seriously, I decided to form my own workshop/seminar company because I had a lot to say about the development of one's potential and how to live up to it. I named my company "Personal Potentials Unlimited." To me, that name said it all. Those three words firmly state that *my* personal potential, *your* personal potential, and the personal potential of *every living being is unlimited.* The concept still excites me.

What happened to Personal Potentials Unlimited? It still exists and I operate under that name today. The problem back then was that I wasn't really sure about which of the many aspects of personal potential that I wanted to talk about and teach. Too much was going on in my mind, too many ideas, thoughts, concepts, philosophies. I felt the need to clarify things, and when I find myself in that position, I turn to writing to figure it all out. What developed is that I not only found it necessary to completely focus my energies on writing in order to clarify my objectives and views, I enjoyed it. In addition to personal potential, I focused on positive thinking. One, two, and then three books emerged as a result.

Later, I realized that being published definitely created credibility, which is of primary concern in the seminar/workshop field. Because I enjoy writing so much, that phase of my career took predominance over the seminars and workshops. Of course, I also conduct these from time to time on the subjects of my books, but writing continues to be my first love.

Potential: It's hidden in what you love to do

What is *your* first love? I'm willing to guess that whatever it is that you like to do—make that *love* to do—is something that you are potentially good at doing. I love to write, I hope I am finally good at it. Even if I weren't, I'd continue doing it. I'd write letters, for example, just because I love to write. I love to communicate my thoughts, feelings, emotions; I love telling little stories—in writing—about my childhood and funny things that happen now, in my mellow adulthood. If you're a personal friend or relative of mine, you're doomed to receive such missives from me every so often, whether you want them or not.

This self-analysis told me that one way to discover your potential is to explore the things you like to do, always wanted to do, or still dream of doing. As an example, let's take the case of a friend I'll call Josephine. I met Josephine many years ago when we both belonged to the same women's group. I was immediately attracted to her because of her vibrant personality and unusual voice; it had character. Naturally, I mentioned this to Josephine, who noted that she'd been told it for years. In fact, she related that it was her dream to use her voice in some productive yet dramatic way, in radio commercials, perhaps, or some other area related to show business.

This excited me because I was in radio management at the time and one of the things I was responsible for was writing and producing the station's commercials. We had an in-house production group, and unlike the way it is today, with advertising agencies handling the majority of accounts and their commercials, our group wrote and produced almost all of the commercial messages we aired. I did the writing, and cast whomever I could find handy to voice the various parts.

So Josephine seemed a natural to join what we called the KRE Little Theater Group. Josephine said she "wasn't ready," that she wanted to take some professional classes in voice, acting, speech modulation, and other areas she felt were necessary before actually getting in front of a microphone. I told her that she had natural potential, that she was perfect just the way she was, and we were ready to utilize her marvelous voice and vibrant personality in our next session. She declined.

Off and on, when we had need of a special voice, my colleague Duncan, who directed the sessions, inquired about Josephine. I told him I'd check with her again, and I always did. During this period, she was taking elocution lessons and said she would let us know when she was ready.

Later, Duncan left to form his own independent production group. It took off like gangbusters and soon he had several major national accounts. He called me to ask about Josephine because he needed a special female voice for a well-known sponsor; evidently I had done a great selling job when describing her gifts in the field of commercials and voice-overs. Now Josephine was taking breathing lessons, but she said she'd let us know when she was ready.

Many years went by. I'd bump into Josephine now and then, or hear about her from mutual friends. She still had her dream about doing something in broadcasting, and she was still taking various lessons.

Then I joined a fun-loving group of broadcasters that calls itself the Broadcast Legends. And that's what they are: old-time broadcasters, many of whom are still active in radio and TV, who get together every couple of months to laugh, reminisce, and, as their motto says, "To have fun with colleagues from the years when broadcasting was fun!" At one of the meetings, I collected business cards of members active in the broadcast area that was of such intense interest to Josephine. They offered to help her in any way they could, and I sent her the information. Again, she declined to follow through; this time she was taking acting lessons.

> *It is very dangerous to go into eternity with possibilities which one has oneself prevented from becoming realities. A possibility is a hint from God. One must follow it.*
>
> —SØREN KIERKEGAARD

All in all, over twenty-five years have passed since I first learned of Josephine's burning desire to capitalize on her unusual voice. I offered her several concrete opportunities to make her dream come true, to actually utilize her fabulous potential and be on the air, first in the San Francisco Bay Area, the fourth largest market in the United States, then to be heard nationwide through association with Duncan's production company. At a recent gathering, she wistfully talked of the career that might have been and seemed doomed to die before it began. I said nothing, but thought of two things. First, my favorite quote of all time:

> *Regret for the things we did can be tempered by time; it is regret for the things we did not do that is inconsolable.*
>
> —SYDNEY J. HARRIS

It is the second line of that quote that really gets to me every time I think of it. It was that line that motivated me to write my first book. If I were Josephine, I would be inconsolable at the thought of going to my grave without having at least given my dream the opportunity to become a reality.

> *Most people go to their graves with their songs still unsung.*
>
> —OLIVER WENDELL HOLMES

The other thing that I thought of as Josephine mourned the impending death of her dream was the old joke that I'm sure you've heard about the very devout man who had an unshakable belief that God would take care of him no matter what catastrophe might befall him.

One day it began to rain in the town where he lived and the nearby rivers overflowed. People fled from their homes as the water rose. His neighbors stopped by in their car on their way to higher ground and urged him to come with them to safety. He replied that God would save him.

It continued to rain and the water continued to rise. The man moved to the second floor of his house. Some people came by in a rowboat and urged him to come with them to safety. He replied that God would save him.

The rains did not diminish. Soon the man was forced to go his rooftop to avoid the rising water. A helicopter flew by and the pilot shouted that he would throw down a line to rescue him. The man replied that God would save him.

Soon the water level rose even higher and the man drowned. When he arrived at the Pearly Gates, God said, "It's not your time. Why are you here?"

The man said, "Why didn't you save me. I believed in You! I waited and waited, but You never came."

God replied, "I sent you a car, a rowboat, and a helicopter. What more did you want?"

You—and only you—can act on your potential

Please, if you have potential—or have been told that you have it in some area—and it's something that lights your fire, *act on it!* Perhaps Josephine felt that by taking lessons for years, she was acting on her dream. Good thinking, but to a limited degree. When *opportunity* knocks on your door, *you must answer and act on it!*

Josephine could have been an active member of our Little Theater Group and *still* taken her private lessons. She could have voiced a part in one of Duncan's national radio or TV spots and *still* taken lessons. She could have talked with professionals in the field who were willing to help her and *still* taken lessons on the side.

I wonder how many elocution, breathing, and acting lessons the old gal took who voiced the memorable line, "Where's the beef?" in the Wendy's commercials. Or the woman who cried, "I've fallen and I can't get up!" Maybe they were seasoned actors from central casting, but I'm sure Josephine could have pulled off a short line like one of those without the need of twenty-five years of lessons. At least she could have taken me up on the many offers and given it the old college try.

In retrospect, I often thought that Josephine was afraid—afraid of succeeding. Now that's a concept that I have never been able to understand, but I hear it frequently occurs with some personality types.

The aim, if reached or not, makes great the life;
Try to be Shakespeare, leave the rest to fate.

—ROBERT BROWNING

My fantastic friend Fred

Josephine's story brings my friend "Fantastic Fred" to mind because he is the exact opposite. Fantastic Fred, sometimes called "Fantastic" for short, is Fred Schiavo, a professional speaker from Rohnert Park, who also runs a leasing company. The first time Fred called me and I inquired who was on the line, he said, "Fantastic. I'm

Fantastic Fred!" After telling him that I was pretty fantastic myself, we got down to the purpose of his call. But not until I told him what a fabulous radio voice he had.

We hit it off so well over the phone that before I knew it, Fred offered to send me a short, true story to include in my book *Putting the Positive Thinker to Work*. It was instantly obvious to me that Fred is a positive thinker of the first order.

Over time and ongoing conversations, we discussed Fred's deep, distinctive voice—actually it's rather sexy. Other than speaking professionally, I asked, what was he doing with it? As with Josephine, Fred had a dream. You guessed it! Fred really, *really* wanted to do voice-overs. (A voice-over, by the way, are the words you hear an announcer speak over something visual on the TV screen, such as the upcoming programming schedule, or almost anything that does not show the actual person speaking.)

To make this part of Fred's story short, Fred will be going to the next Broadcast Legends meeting as my guest, at which time I'll be able to introduce him to others already in the field. He has the potential, and he is not afraid to act on what might be a golden opportunity.

And because Fred always has a meaningful story to offer, I'll hand the microphone, so to speak, over to him right now. Here's Fred:

As a kid, I had a pretty bad self-image. I believed that I was stupid and would never amount to anything. I was barely out of high school when World War II ended and I was drafted into the army and required to take an IQ test. Since I graduated with a C average, taking that test really concerned me. I believed I would fail and end up in the infantry.

All two hundred men in our company took the test at the same time. When we completed it, our commanding officer came out of his office and called us all to attention and said, "Will the following three men step forward." He called out three names and mine was one of them. I was absolutely terrified, holding to the belief that we were probably the dumbest in the whole company. He then asked us to follow him to his office. As soon as we were seated, he announced, "You three men scored the highest in the company in your tests. I suggest you consider going to officers' candidate school.

That moment changed my life! For the first time, someone was actually telling me that I wasn't stupid, that I was really smart, that I had potential! That I was *one of three* chosen over several hundred others as having a higher-than-average IQ. And they wanted me to consider going to officers' candidate school!

I chose not to go to OCS because I wasn't interested in a long-term commitment or becoming a career soldier. Instead, because of my background as a choir singer in high school, my appearance as a soft-shoe dancer in a neighborhood revue, and my Abbott and Costello skits with my brother at Bond Rallies, I was assigned to a soldier show called *Sharps & Flats*. I sang bass in a quartet and was also in the chorus. We toured throughout Germany and Austria, presenting our show to GI audiences.

While on tour, I met a stage hypnotist who was assigned to our outfit. After watching him perform and meeting with him, I decided to read every book I could find on hypnosis and other self-help books. After the positive experience with the test score, and reading dozens of self-help books, I decided that I had it in *me* to change my life. Freddie was ready!

In my quest to improve my self-esteem and self-image, I continued to read self-help books. In one, I came across a reference in an essay by William James, former professor at Harvard University, to something called the "as if" principle. James said: "If you act as if you have a quality, you will get it." Based on his principle, I believed that if I acted fantastic every day, I would be fantastic. So every time someone asked me how I was, I would answer by saying, "Fantastic!"

One day a guy asked me how I was, and when I replied "Fantastic!" he said, "Fred you can't be fantastic every day." "You're right," I replied in a subdued tone, "some days I'm fantastic. And," I bellowed, "some days I'M FANTASTIC!" It wasn't long before people started calling me Fantastic Fred, and they still do to this day.

Our self-image and our habits tend to go together. Change one and you will automatically change the other.

—DR. MAXWELL MALTZ

Affirmations and the "as if" principle

I've discused the "as if" principle before, but I'd like to remind you of it again right now because it can help you immeasurably when it comes to reaching your true potential.

The "as if" principle is the basis of the Law of Expectation, which says that what you expect and believe with confidence will tend to materialize. What you believe becomes your reality. The idea is to act "as if" your expectation has already come to pass. You must put the cart before the horse, so to speak. And because there is a definite causal link between belief and behavior, your expectation and belief *determine* your behavior.

When Fred declared, "I'm fantastic," he *expected* to be fantastic; he *believed* he was fantastic; he *acted* fantastic; he *behaved* "as if" he were fantastic. Therefore, over time, Fred actually *became* fantastic.

The "as if" principle is also an important component of all affirmations, or goal-oriented statements. Affirmations are statements that are constructed in a positive manner, in the present tense, as if the result were an actuality, with goals being definite, not vague. Perhaps when Fred first started saying, "I'm fantastic," he may have had some nagging doubts in his mind about how fantastic he really was. But over time, when his "I'm fantastic" statement, or affirmation, was repeated endlessly, as must be done with affirmations in order for them to be effective, his subconscious mind accepted his "I'm fantastic" statement as a fact, and Fred followed through by believing, acting, and behaving as if he were fantastic. Fred became fantastic!

Here is my favorite personal "as if" story, which proves the effectiveness of affirmations and the Law of Expectation theory. Some years ago, in the mid-eighties, I was developing my Personal Power Plan, or PPP, which I wrote about extensively in *The Positive Thinker*.

My burning desire and main goal was to be a published author. So I wrote the following affirmation, or statement, in the present tense; my goal was definite, not vague, and it was stated as if the result were an actuality: "I am a published author."

Note that "I am" is in the present tense; I did not say, "I hope to be," "I'd like to be," or "One of these days I'm going to be a published author," which are all vague or in the future tense, not definite. I said, "I am a published author." The affirmation was stated "as if" it were an actuality.

I incorporated that affirmation with the others in my PPP and said and listened to it several times daily in the months that followed. It went deeply into my subconscious mind, as it was supposed to, and my subconscious mind went to work on me. It said, "If you're an author, what have you written?" Well, I had to start producing something to quiet my nagging subconscious mind, so I headed for the typewriter to put my many thoughts on paper. Thankfully, a computer came into my life shortly thereafter, or this story may have ended right there!

After I had the beginnings of a manuscript, my subconscious mind reminded me that I stated that I was a *published* author, and asked, "What are you doing about getting published?" Again, I was forced to act. So I started sending out book proposals, which included my partial manuscript, to publishers. Of course I received many rejections, but by this time I was determined. After all, because of the "as if" principle, I expected, believed, acted, and behaved as if I were a published author. My inner self and subconscious mind said to me: "I am a published author," and published authors are published, right? So I persevered. Six months later, I received the most wonderful telephone call of my life. My editor called and said, "I want to buy your book!" The book turned out to be *The Positive Thinker*, which, at present, is in its sixth printing.

Fred had the potential to be fantastic. Now he is. I had the potential to be a published author. Now I am. What is it that you really want to do, become, or accomplish above all else? Utilize the "as if" principle. Put your goal or dream into affirmation form. Then make a commitment to yourself to follow through by doing what you have to do to live up to your affirmation, because if you don't do your part, your subconscious will lose confidence in you. It cannot accomplish monumental goals and help you reach your unlimited potential without your cooperation. Think of your subconscious mind as a giant within you. It is your obedient servant. Properly guided, it can and will cause miracles to happen. Guide your giant with affirmations and the "as if" principle. Awaken your giant by expecting, believing, acting, and behaving as if you are living up to your potential.

There is a giant asleep within every man. When the giant awakes, miracles happen.

—FREDERICK FAUST

On being different and comfortable with ourselves

Recently, I talked with Michael Lee, an Asian-American colleague from the National Speakers Association, about goals and potential. Michael told me what

it was like to feel different, the importance of being realistic, and learning to be comfortable with ourselves and
who we are. Here's Michael's story:

> I was made not to feel comfortable with myself from
> a very early age. As a young boy, my parents told
> me that because this is America, I could do anything
> I wanted. I quickly learned that while this is the land
> of opportunity, each of us faces unique obstacles in
> achieving our goals. Like most kids, one of my ear-
> liest goals was to belong to a group, and I looked
> forward to the day when I would be old enough to
> go to grammar school.
>
> Finally, the big day came, and wearing my stiff
> new jeans and carrying a Superman lunch box, I was
> sent off by my mother to my first day of kindergar-
> ten. I looked forward to joining my classmates, but
> instead was greeted with a chorus of "Ching Chong
> Chinaman." For the first time, I became aware that I
> was different from the other children. At the time, I
> didn't realize that I was not alone. *We are all differ-
> ent in different ways, and because of that, we are the
> same.* Some people are too short, too tall, too fat, too
> skinny, wear glasses, or are somehow different from
> the mythical norm.
>
> To show the other kids that I was just as good as
> they were, I studied very hard and excelled academ-
> ically. I even won a national book-reading contest
> and was the valedictorian of my graduating class.
> While I still didn't feel as if I belonged, I felt vin-
> dicated. I learned judo by correspondence course and
> got good enough to teach it to my classmates. Learn-

ing judo not only helped me belong, it allowed me to excel as well.

In the late 1970s, I set one of my most ambitious goals. After graduating from San Francisco State University and working as a producer for the ABC television network, I decided I wanted to be a movie actor. I studied at the Lee Strassberg Theater Institute and the American Conservatory Theater in San Francisco. Then came acting in regional theater and endless auditions.

While I aspired to be the next Clint Eastwood, I was cast in such roles as karate instructor or Asian gang member. Besides being stereotypes, these roles don't require a whole lot of acting skills. I didn't want to be an Asian actor, but rather an actor who just happened to be Asian. I did manage to land a few minor nonstereotypical roles in a couple of films, but parts were few and far between and I got tired of waiting for the phone to ring, so I stopped acting. To survive during those lean years, I got a real-estate license and liked the flexibility of that profession because I could work when available, and refer clients to other agents when I was booked.

It was an enormous letdown to give up acting because it was the thing I most enjoyed doing in life. However, I had to be realistic, because even today, Asians rarely appear in other than stereotypical roles on TV and in films.

In the eighties, I taught television production at community colleges, and before long, I was teaching communications and marketing at several universities. I thought the perfect teaching job would be one that was flexible enough to allow me to travel the world. This led to the world of professional speaking, which, in addition to teaching and travel, can pay extremely well.

I wanted to be the next Tony Robbins, one of our great motivational speakers. Unfortunately, every time I spoke on motivation or other common topics like time management or negotiation, people always asked me to speak on the subject of diversity and culture because I'm a fifth-generation Asian American whose family has been in the United States since the 1880s.

I gave in and started giving classes on how to sell real estate to Asian clients. Then a new-car dealer asked me to do a program on multicultural car buyers. Eventually, I developed different programs for different industries and different cultures. In this area, I have very little competition; speaking on culture makes me unique.

Over the years, I have learned that being different is okay and I now embrace that difference. It has its advantages: people tend to remember me since I am probably the first Asian-American speaker they've seen; the minute I walk onto the platform I have instant credibility; plus I have no competition.

If you've ever felt different, and haven't we all, heed what Michael has to say and embrace your difference rather than fighting it. Remember, we are all different in one way or another and that actually makes us alike. Emphasize and capitalize on your uniqueness; it can help you find and capitalize on your potential, just as Michael did.

Be realistic

An important part of Michael's message is to be realistic. Here is one of the most drop-dead gorgeous men I've ever met, definitely leading-man material. But Hollywood insisted on casting him in stereotypical roles. So Michael became realistic and set about determining what he could do that would work and still give him the personal satisfaction that he deserved in his career.

He found it in professional speaking. As a professional speaker, Michael has what most actors can only dream of. He writes his own material, so he believes implicitly in what he says. He is confident with himself and his diversity. He puts on a one-man show and has the stage, or platform, to himself, so he is never upstaged. He always has an attentive audience. And he receives appreciative applause. In addition, he is well paid. As the song says, "Who can ask for anything more?" Michael summed up his message to me with these words:

Obstacles are what make us successful. Overcoming them makes us unique and stronger.

Today I teach people to value their differences. Take an interest in other people's differences. Remember that treating people equally is not necessarily treating people fairly. We must adapt to others. We must try to live up to our potential. We are all born with unlimited potential. However, that inner core is hidden by layers of social, political, physical, and other factors which can slow our progress toward reaching that potential. Each of us must learn to peel away each limiting layer to get to the center of our true potential.

All the wonders you seek are within yourself.
—SIR THOMAS BROWNE

Do whatever it takes

A couple of weeks ago, I received a package in the mail that absolutely thrilled me to pieces. It was a book from my friend Amy Berger. I knew Amy was working on a book, but I didn't realize the project had actually come to fruition, so it was a real joy to hold her "baby" in my hands. We all consider our books our babies, and when one is finally published, it's as if we've personally given birth.

Early on in her project, Amy had asked me if I knew anyone who might be appropriate to illustrate her book-in-progress and I happily recommended my very dear friend Elena Facciola, who illustrated and definitely enhanced my first two books. According to Amy's description of her project, Elena seemed absolutely perfect. So I had the double pleasure of reading Amy's book and seeing Elena's amusing sketches.

Naturally, I wanted to know all about Amy's experience from beginning to end. Amy complied with my request by sending the following personal story to me:

In late 1996, at two P.M on a Thursday evening, I attended a seminar that changed my life. The presenter was author Hal Zina Bennett, who had just published a book entitled *How to Write from the Heart*. During the next three hours, I decided that I had a book inside me that longed to be written, hired Hal's wife, Susan Sparrow, to be my writing coach, and started my journey.

Working with my new coach, I quickly learned that I already possessed the basic ingredients of a writer—good grammar and sentence-structure capabilities and, most important of all, something to say. I worked with Susan over the next fourteen months as she helped me pull forth a two-hundred-page humor book which I lovingly titled *The Twenty Year Itch: Confessions of a Corporate Warrior*. Writing the book over the course of 1997 was not the hard part. I love to write and have done it consistently in my "real" jobs over the past several years. Sitting down to formulate each chapter in the wee hours of the morning before work or on many a Saturday morning was pure joy.

As the manuscript was nearing completion, I was advised that it was time to find a publishing company that could take up my cause. From Susan and some local seminars I learned the process of soliciting a commitment from an editor, literary agent, or publisher. I spoke with friends and colleagues who'd recently published books to get contact names. During the course of the next fourteen months, I rode an emotional roller coaster that was often very painful. After handcrafting over thirty-five query letters, packaging each one with a book proposal or manuscript, and sending them across the country, I was left with a myriad of rejection letters. The entire process was extremely disheartening. At times, it was hard to hold on to my dream of having my book published.

In mid-1998, I decided it was time to put myself out of my misery and give myself a gift—literally. I had maintained a growing savings account for a few years and knew that there was enough money in it to cover the cost of printing five-hundred books. Although it was not my first intention to use the money for book publishing, I knew I had to commit those resources in order to put my mind—and soul—to rest. I knew the book was a special one; that was confirmed to me by nearly forty friends and acquaintances who read the manuscript. I was like a dog with a bone and strongly believed I needed to finish what I started. I knew I couldn't rest until I felt my manuscript in my hands, in *real* book form, and beheld its fresh "hot off the press" smell. I couldn't and wouldn't let the project go until the book was published.

It took me roughly six months to chose and hire a printer, illustrator, editor, and graphic artist. After the editing, cover, and illustrations were complete, I did all the formatting myself to save money. I had been laid off from my corporate job just weeks before, so finances were even more of a concern. My husband said I could continue with my self-publishing plan if I got a consulting client by the month's end. Otherwise we'd have to postpone the printing of *The Twenty Year Itch*. Fortunately, the angels heard my prayers, because a client and his first paycheck kept the book project on schedule. I hated the tedious work of text formatting, but my clear vision of my *published* book kept me going. Luckily, my husband was available to help me with some last-minute illustration preparation work that needed to be done.

Finally, on January 13, 1999, I sent the entire package to my printers in Ohio. By February 23 I had my "baby" in my hands—all five-hundred of them. An incredible sense of relief and accomplishment washed over me as I held that first copy in my palms and brought it up to my nostrils. I had done it! I was in print after all. I still don't know the fate of *The Twenty Year Itch,* but I do know that I was meant to write it and publish it. With the sweet smell of success still lingering, I feel as if I have just climbed Mount Everest or rafted down the length of the Colorado River. I can breathe easy for the first time in nearly three years and it feels wonderful.

Isn't that a wonderful, inspiring story? Amy literally did *whatever it takes* to get her dream book out of her head and into print.

Act on your dream

What is your dream? Please know that if you do whatever it takes, your dream *will*—note I did not say can, I said *will*—become a reality. Amy could have quit after the fun part, that of writing, which, for her, was pure joy. The tedious part was the rest of it. And that's where most of us fall down on the job. We do not follow through and do whatever it takes. We don't persevere, persist, and go the extra mile. We shrug our shoulders and say, "It just didn't work," and we give up. Amy didn't allow that to happen to her. Amy did whatever it takes. Amy hung in there and, finally, she was rewarded with the gold ring, the Oscar, the ultimate prize. Amy saw her dream come to fruition. That is why I was so thrilled when I received Amy's book in the mail. Because I've been there as well. I could appreciate her "baby" as if it were my own.

Today, take a first small step to live up to your potential. Determine what it is you are good at doing, and what you really, *really* want to do. Say, "I can do that," and then start to do it. Utilize the "as if" principle. Embrace your individual differences. Be realistic. If you get bogged down along the way, remember Amy and do whatever it takes. And don't ever, *ever* think about stopping until you reach your goal, your personal potential.

> *Do little things in an extraordinary way. You must not let your life run in the ordinary way; do something that will dazzle the world. Show that God's creative principle works in you. Never mind the past. Have the unflinching determination to move on your path unhampered by limiting thoughts of past errors.*
>
> —PARAMAHANSA YOGANANDA

To answer the three questions posed in the beginning of this chapter about personal potential—although by now you may have additional insights—consider these answers:

> *Where is personal potential to be found?* It is found within.
>
> *How can we recognize it?* It is something that we love to do, are compelled to do, and are good at doing.
>
> *How do we release it?* We release it simply by doing. We listen to our intuition and impulses. We open

the door when opportunity knocks. And we *act*!
Remember, nothing happens without action.

All the wonders you seek are within yourself.

—SIR THOMAS BROWNE

My Resolutions

In regard to Commandment VI, *Live Up to Your Potential and Do Whatever It Takes,* these are my resolutions:

....
....
....
....
....
....
....
....
....
....
....
....
....
....
....
....
....
....
....
....
....
....

Communicate Effectively in All Areas of Life

Sticks and stones may break my bones, but words can never hurt me.

—Old childhood saying

WRONG! Absolutely wrong, wrong, wrong! Words can be lethal. When used as weapons, words can inflict wounds that, if allowed to fester, may never heal. As Robert Burton said in The Anatomy of Melancholy, "A blow with a word strikes deeper than a blow with a sword."

As humans, our primary means of communication is through words. Spoken words, written words, and in this era of technology, electronic words. Usually we know what we *mean* to say, but how are our words interpreted? Often they are misunderstood. We respond to what we think we *heard* rather than to what was actually *said*.

Innocent comments and their unexpected effects

As a writer, and one who relies on the use of words in my work as well as my personal life, I am keenly aware of the power of both the spoken and written word. Yet I am constantly astounded by the number of times I am misunderstood because of the improper way I phrased innocent comments. Let me give you examples of three recent faux pas:

I was gifted with a new mini–kitchen TV for my birthday. I mentioned this to my sister and her daughter when they called to congratulate me on my special day. I noted to them that because rabbit ears are passé, it is no longer possible to simply plug a TV into an electrical outlet and expect to get a picture; the TV must be hooked up to a cable system in order to generate an image.

Cheryl, my niece, said that's not a problem, and she expounded on the proper method of splicing wires and connecting them to other cable-connected household TVs in order to achieve the desired results. I was both amused and amazed at her knowledge, but told her to hold the technicalities because there was no way I was going to undertake such a procedure myself. In addition, I didn't want wires strung along the floorboards and over doorways, which was the method that my sister, who also unexpectedly had knowledge in the area, suggested.

So they both advised me to talk to Cheryl's husband, David, who was standing by the phone and who would be pleased to give me step-by-step instructions. I said, "Don't even bother putting David on the phone. I don't have any intention of doing this myself, I'll hire someone. David is a handyman and smart along such lines, whereas I am a total klutz in this area."

Cheryl was instantly offended by my use of the word "handyman." "David is *not* just a handyman, he's a Ph.D candidate, a producer of film documentaries, and . . ." She went on to recount his many talents. My sister tactfully changed the subject at this point and it wasn't until after I hung up that I realized how deeply my innocent yet inappropriate use of the term "handyman" had offended Cheryl. She was sensitive because David is the superintendent of a large, luxurious apartment building in an exclusive suburban area and she took my statement to mean that he was *simply* a handyman, or as *Webster* defines the term, "a man who does odd jobs." Roget, on the other hand, in his *International Thesaurus*, equates handyman with such terms as "proficient, expert, adept, professional, authority, and efficiency expert," among other glowing qualifications.

I instantly wrote Cheryl a two-page letter of apology. I explained that to me, the term "handyman" was meant in a complimentary, rather than a derogatory, way. I mentioned several men in our family who had handyman talents and capabilities along with their other attributes, as well as those who would never dare put the term "handyman" on their résumés. My late husband, a military pilot by profession, was a fine handyman; my son, an attorney, inherited his father's handyman talents; my father, Cheryl's grandfather, was a banker and a financial whiz, but definitely *not* a handyman; and Hans, my close friend, a marathoner, cyclist, and tour guide who does many things extremely well, also could never qualify to wear a hat bearing the title "handyman."

Cheryl got back to me to say she was tired the day

we spoke and apologized for flying off the handle. While I hope she really understood, I promised myself to be more careful of my words henceforth. Then I did it again—inadvertently, of course.

I had placed an ad in a publication that goes to radio and television producers nationwide, in hopes of generating interviews for my third book, which had recently been released. One of the first responses I received was from Annette, who called to set up a series of interviews with John, her boss and associate, who hosts a talk show at a northern Michigan radio station. Over the course of the several conversations and faxes that went back and forth, Annette and I became quite friendly, and when I wrote to John with the background information he requested, I complimented him on his choosing such an enthusiastic sidekick and supporter to be his assistant.

The next time I talked with Annette, she seemed disturbed and I finally got her to confess that she was hurt because I demoted her to "sidekick," a term that she did not like or appreciate. In amazement, I explained that the term "sidekick" was meant as a compliment. Roget defines sidekick as "confederate, partner, comrade, associate, colleague" and other terms, all positive. I was thinking of such partnerships as Burns and Allen, Abbott and Costello, Astaire and Rogers, the Lone Ranger and Tonto, among other well-known teams. It took a bit of persuasion to convince Annette that my use of sidekick was more of a promotion to the status of equal partner than a demotion to a subordinate role.

Are you ready for one more of Alice's thoughtless foot-in-the-mouth gaffes? My friend Beverly, with whom I worked in the sixties; called to invite me to lunch to celebrate my birthday. We have kept in touch over the years and routinely get together on birthdays, as well as anytime either one of us can dream up an excuse for a special lunch. I gladly accepted. Then, when Beverly mentioned that her daughter, Connie, who is also my good friend, hoped to join us, I said, "Wonderful! Connie *really* knows how to celebrate and make any occasion a special one."

Beverly was silent for a moment; then she said in a subdued tone, "You mean *I* don't?" "Uh-oh," I said to myself. "I've done it again!" What I meant was that when one goes out to lunch with Connie, there are no holds barred. She orders everything on the menu, or at least something from every category from appetizer to dessert for all to share, with appropriate wines throughout. When I dine with Beverly alone, as with most of my other friends, the diet of the day or week often takes precedence over menu preferences as we struggle to maintain willpower and resist temptation. Certainly, no one would ever consider ordering more than one course. As for dessert? Never!

Small stuff, too insignificant to mention? Not necessarily. Sometime the small slings and arrows, if not explained and clarified, are the ones that fester, cause misunderstanding, and eventually do us in. The offhand remark, so innocent and unimportant at the time of utterance, becomes indelibly recorded on one's mental tape to be repeated ad infinitum.

> *Once a word has been allowed to escape, it can never be recalled.*
>
> —HORACE

Culture and communication

Sometimes it's a difference in culture that can cause a lack of communication and thus misunderstanding. My friend and colleague Craig Harrison, a fellow member of National Speakers Association who speaks on communication skills, sent me this story after a conversation on the subject.

In the summer of 1993, I coached a boys basketball team for the international nonprofit Sports for Understanding. I assembled a collection of high-school boys from around the United States and we traveled to Australia to play basketball against Australian teams of high-schoolers for part of June and much of July, living with host families, playing basketball, and touring the country. A similar team of American girls toured with us, with their own coach. We traveled together and played our games the same days or nights.

My boys were excited to visit a foreign country. For many, it was their first time out of the U.S. For one, a freshman, it was his first time away from Lake Oswego, Oregon. One young man came from the mean streets of Boston, another from the suburbs of Orinda, California. One came from a small town in West Virginia and another from a Jesuit school in Detroit.

Many funny things happened on this trip. Because we shared a common language with the Australians, we were unprepared for one particular misunderstanding that concerned the parents that were hosting us.

We had just won one of our first games. My players were huddled around me for instructions as to what to do next. The Australian parents and their kids who were hosting our boys were also gathered around the huddle to learn what we were going to do next.

Full of adrenaline and excitement, I commended the team on their good play and teamwork, and reminded them how, in team sports, we win as a team and lose as a team. Now that our game had concluded, I felt it only appropriate to stay and support the girls' team, which was to play in a few minutes.

So I led us in a cheer, "All for one and one for all," and then said in a loud voice so all our players and host parents could hear, "Now let's go root on the girls!"

Our guys cheered and started running toward the court where the girls were warming up. The host families suddenly expressed looks of horror. One woman shrieked. Another clutched her daughter to her and covered her ears as if to shield her from my words. Some of the fathers started to snicker and cast sideways glances at each other. These were the same parents who had previously welcomed me and my group into their homes with open arms, having their children pose with us for photos.

I knew something was wrong but didn't know what. Little did I know that "root on" is Australian slang for having relations with someone. I had just advocated our team's engaging in sexual activities with the girls. Oops!

By the end of the trip, we all had a keen appreciation for the many sayings that carry different meanings between our languages. In England and Australia, when you visit somebody, you "knock them up." In our country, that same expression refers to what can happen after you "root on" somebody— They can get pregnant!

Some innocuous words of ours have differing meanings. For instance, the word "ring" in Australian slang refers to one's rear aperture. Conversely, the word "fag" in Australia refers to cigarettes and is heard often. In Australia, kiwis aren't fruits, they're New Zealanders.

We found out the hard way that even when words share the same letters and sounds, they can confer different meanings. Everywhere we went we ordered milkshakes. Never did we actually receive the type of thick drink we've grown accustomed to in the States. Australian shakes were thin and runny. Then again, we found things we preferred over their American counterparts.

All in all, our trip gave us a great appreciation for differences and similarities between the cultures, whether in communication, custom, or even style of play in basketball.

Our counterparts were thrilled to learn American slang and have us decipher songs they'd heard whose words they couldn't understand. We all benefited from our cross-cultural experience and made many new friends. With basketball as our common language, we communicated many universal truths!

The chief merit of language is clarity, and we know that nothing detracts so much from this as do unfamiliar terms.

—GALEN

Craig had another, rather humorous lack-of-communication story to share. He told me of the time he went to the dentist to have his wisdom teeth removed. He was given the usual novocaine, as well as a pill to calm him because he was nervous. So he was in a state of semiconsciousness when, with mouth wide open, he heard the dentist request a "two-by-four." Craig imagined a huge piece of wood being readied for insertion into his mouth; actually a two-by-four, in dental parlance, is a piece of gauze two inches by four inches. And then, when the dentist requested an "explorer," Craig was ready to bolt from the chair regardless of the two-by-fours and other items cluttering his mouth.

The problem was lack of communication on the part of the dentist; he should have prepared Craig in advance for all aspects of the procedure. As it was, in his dazed state, and without sufficient preparation about what he might expect, Craig said he was literally terrified!

Craig's mother, Evalee Harrison, who is well-known in these parts for her radio and television programs promoting physical fitness as well as her popular newspaper columns on the same subject, also offered an amusing anecdote on the subject of communication and the lack of it.

Evalee was hosting a TV show called *Take a Break*. At the commencement of filming one day, the cameraman asked the director, "What's next?" The director replied, *"Take a Break."* And so the cameraman did just that. He took a break and didn't return until his usual break time of twenty minutes was up! Unfortunately, all production came to a halt until the cameraman returned! Yes, lack of communication can have its humorous moments!

Even the Gods love their jokes.

—PLATO

By definition, communication is the ability of one person to make contact with another and to make himself understood. S. I. Hayakawa states that "Language is an effective medium of communicating, but only when the speaker or writer is able to convey a message, to get across what he means. A person speaking Spanish, for example, is unable to communicate with a person who speaks only English. And an expert who may have an impressive command of technical jargon may lack the broad-based language skills needed to communicate knowledge to laymen. One may communicate, however, not only through speech or writing but also through looks or gestures, signals or codes. In a more sophisticated sense, *communicate* stresses the technological transmission of information or ideas. Men now communicate over long distances by means of telephone, telegraph, radio, television, and satellite."

Four-legged communicators

Animals are great communicators, utilizing their unique kinds of looks, gestures, signals, and codes. Paul, one of my pen pals, sent me this observation:

It is interesting to me that cats and dogs learn how to "talk" to us humans. My cat (we have been together for 12 years) can read my mind like a book. He knows just how to get whatever he wants. For example, his food dish is empty and I am not paying attention to that fact. First he will go and sit quietly by his dish looking hopefully in my direction. He will give this about 15 minutes, and if I do not respond correctly, his next move is to go over to the good sitting chair, stretch out his two front legs onto the side of the chair, and prepare to CLAW! But he doesn't, he simply turns his head in my direction to see if I am watching (I am), and as I rush over to fill his dish with goodies, this cat knows that he has communicated his wants to me! How effective and direct! How did this cat learn that he can badger his master into filling his food dish? I don't know, but it works.

This amused me greatly because my cat, PK, is also a marvelous communicator. When the level in her food dish reaches the halfway point, she paces back and forth in front of it. If I don't notice or seem to ignore the situation, she does her pleading "roll over" number in front of the dish, a move designed to cajole me into acceding to her wishes. If that gets no action, a paw, with claws extended, will lash out in my direction accompanied by loud, impatient, angry meows. She succeeds in getting my attention, and as in the case of Paul's cat, her wants taken care of.

My dog, Charlie, on the other hand, is more direct and forceful in his communication. Sometimes he will undertake the expectant look-and-wait bit, which seems to work with the cats, but most of the time, he hurls, leaps, or barges with, as I said, unexpected force.

Charlie and PK each have their own personal territories in the house; Charlie spends most of his time in the bedroom and back half of the house, and PK has the kitchen, family room, and the bathroom in which her litter box is located. When Charlie wants company, a snack, or to go out in the yard, and I am not nearby, he knocks on the bedroom door with his paw, then sits back expectantly, waiting for the door to be opened. After a few minutes, if there is no response, he takes more drastic measures and hurls himself against the door in order to get my attention. This causes a loud crashing noise that is audible anywhere in the house. I'm used to Charlie's method of communication, of course, but when I have company, this thunderous noise can really startle them!

And when Charlie wants to play ball, he'll drag a variety of balls out of his basket and display them in front of me. If I don't respond quickly enough, he'll pick up the ball of his choice and hurl himself against me! This little twenty-pound fluffball can pack quite a wallop, I'll tell you! "I want to play ball, Mom. And I want you to play ball with me, *now*," is his message. Yes, Charlie. I get it, loud and clear!

This communication between dog and master goes two ways and I'm pleased to report that Charlie understands a great deal of what is said to him. He is very proud to be asked or told to guard the house, for example. When I'm ready to go out, I simply say, "Mommy's going out and Charlie is guarding the house." He instantly jumps up on his love seat, where he has a clear view of the yard and the critters that roam there, and occasional humans that appear, and assumes his "on guard" position. The gardeners and meter readers are terrified by this twenty-pound sentry with a bark that should emanate from a pit bull or rottweiler. And he knows to run and get his harness and leash when I ask, "Does Charlie want to go for a walk?"

The best thing about animals is that they don't talk much.

—THORNTON WILDER

An unusual method of human communication

Paul, my cat-owner friend, laments that we as humans, with our supposedly highly developed language skills, are often not as direct as animals in our attempts at communication. He blames social conditioning, saying, "We're taught to be polite and semiformal from a very early age and this leads to poor communication in adult life. Many people live in two worlds, the outward facade they present, and the inner one of their thoughts and feelings. Some, sadly, can never bring the two together, and when in close relationships, they continue this 'game,' never really communicating what they truly feel in their inner world."

Paul continued, "Words mean different things to different people. The same word used one way by a person speaking can be interpreted in a completely different way by the listener." How true, as shown by my "handyman" and "sidekick" gaffes! Paul suggests that people who are close, and those who spend a lot of time together, devise a system that can give a clue as to the emotional state at any given moment because we often feel the need to hide attitudes of sadness, anger, or other emotions from ones we love. Paul gave me this example of a successful system devised by a couple he knew well:

I had a second set of parents, Abe and Eve, whom I adopted when I was around twenty. I admired them because they made a good team, working hard toward a common goal and what they both wanted in life. They ran a summer farm camp, and in the winter months, they were simply "hoedown dirt farmers," as we called such people when I was growing up in Michigan. They both loved the demanding routine of running the camp in the summer and working the farm in winter. I used to go to their place often in the winter months on the weekend to help out and spend time in the country.

One evening, Abe and I had just finished chores and, exhausted, made our way back to the farmhouse. As we got to the door of the kitchen, Abe stopped me and said, "Before we go in, let me open the door a crack and I'll pitch my hat in." I wondered what that was for, and Abe quickly explained in an earnest tone, "If the hat comes back out, we need to go find something else to do for a half hour. And if the hat does not come back out, then we can go in." When I seemed puzzled, Abe continued his explanation. "If Eve has had a hard day in the kitchen and tending to the house, she may want a few moments to sit and collect herself before she needs to hear what we've been up to!"

Abe and Eve had a unique communication system that worked for them. I knew them for thirty-five years and I never saw them in a heated argument or

even the smallest tiff. Of course they had disagree-
ments, but that little hat signal took the pressure off
the stresses that might have escalated into something
major. I think all husbands and wives need to work
out their own set of signals for times when it's best
to communicate without words.

*Speech was given to the ordinary sort of men
whereby to communicate their mind, but to wise
men, whereby to conceal it.*

—ROBERT SOUTHEY

Communicating in relationships

For relationships to survive for thirty-five years, as
did Abe and Eve's, communication is not a luxury, it is
a must. In this respect, communication refers to an act
of sharing; it's often been called the lifeline of love. If
we've shared our thoughts, feelings, and emotions and
the response is positive, if the recipient *understands,* we
can assume we have something in common. Actually,
what we have shared is *ourselves*. This takes brutal honesty and puts us in a state of vulnerability. We worry:
Will we be accepted, laughed at, ridiculed? If we truly
wish to share in an open honest manner, are we ready
to expose our fears and weaknesses—our dark side?
Will we be as accepting of our partner's openness as we
expect him to be of ours? Is it better to communicate
only to a limited degree in order to reserve some privacy, to erect a safety zone, no matter how slim, between
us?

It is important to understand that when we communicate in a loving, intimate way with a person close to us—or even when we communicate in an honest way in a less-than-intimate situation because we want our real selves to be known and understood—we are offering ourselves as gifts to the listener. And we must also understand that when someone opens herself up to us, she is offering herself as a gift to us as well. This exchange is what we call *personal* communication.

And this communication must be treated with the greatest care and respect in the world. It must never be abused or mistreated. Also, communication of this sort must never be used as a means of causing guilt or eliciting pity or sympathy. Nor should it raise the slightest possibility of rejection, ridicule, or condemnation on the part of either party. True understanding must be above such ploys.

> *That which we understand we can't blame.*
>
> —GOETHE

As I am writing this chapter, I am undergoing one of the most challenging periods of my life. Communication seem to have broken down, if it ever existed at all. Although I have been earnestly striving to make my feelings and concerns known to someone close to me, I feel as if I've hit a brick wall. Long ago I learned that not everyone wants, or has the skills, to openly communicate. But my head and heart scream, "Listen to me! Let me share my innermost thoughts with you! Please, try to understand what it feels like to be me! And let me tune into what it's like to be you. Tell me about your hopes and dreams; share your fears, hurts, and concerns with me. I *do* care because I love you."

When I receive little or no response, or a stony silence, I do what I've always done when it seems useless to continue trying to convey my thoughts, feelings, and emotions out loud: I write to those involved. Long, passionate letters in some cases; short and to the point missives in others. This usually surprises most recipients, or at least it takes them off guard. Since most people have a tremendous aversion to writing anything, especially something extremely personal, or something they think can be cleared up in a brief exchange of words, receiving a carefully thought-out document outlining one's most intimate and personal thoughts, plus an analysis of all sides of the situation, comes as a great surprise. And a revelation. Sometimes it's more than they care to handle. Utilizing this method of communication is not for everyone, but it definitely brings the problem to a head and, sometimes, to a solution.

One time, many years ago, I undertook an extensive series of aptitude tests that were overseen by the Veterans Administration. Since I was a military widow, I was entitled to educational benefits provided by the government and the tests were to determine my strong points and suggest the best direction for my successful future. The results of my VA tests astounded me. If you are unclear about your future path, you, too, may want to consider taking some aptitude tests. I was told that I had a strong desire to perform, on one hand, and on the other, with my rational, analytical mind and ability to see things from both sides, I had all the attributes to be an attorney. It was suggested that by combining the two, I'd make a fine trial lawyer! Well, trial lawyers *do* need exceptional communication skills, don't they!

No, I am not an attorney and, despite the test results, never desired to be one, but my son is. Maybe it's in the genes. But I can be analytical at times, and that comes out in these written, heartfelt communications. You might like to consider this approach if, as with my situation, face-to-face communication seems to fail in your personal relationships.

Putting your thoughts, feelings, and emotions, and possibly an analysis of the situation, in writing is a very valuable exercise, especially if you're confused or uncertain as to your true feelings. It tends to clarify things. Put it all down on paper. Let it sit for a while. Only send or deliver it to the person or persons involved if you feel confident that you've expressed yourself in the way that you wish, and that the document is neutral. By that I mean that it is not sarcastic, derogatory, hateful, or challenging. Ambrose Bierce said, "Speak when you are angry and you will make the best speech you will ever regret." I'll alter that slightly to say, "Write when you are angry and you'll compose the best letter you will ever regret." So, *don't* mail, deliver, or in any way send your communication until you're sure you'll have no regrets about its contents. It may be that by putting your innermost thoughts, feelings, and concerns down on paper, you'll find there's no need to mail or deliver the message. This exercise can be quite therapeutic. According to the headline of a "Your Health" article in the April 26, 1999, issue of *Newsweek*, CONFESSIONAL WRITING CAN BE GOOD FOR YOU. I believe it.

I was concerned about the mighty duo, communication and relationships, and so I thought I'd have a chat with Dolores, a fellow author, who writes relationships books. Her work is filled with personal stories, as are mine. In addition to discussing the communication problem in relationships, I asked her where she gets some of her material.

> Recently, a lot of it has come from the Personals [she told me over lunch]. When I broke up with Jack after eighteen years of togetherness, I was distraught. I put everything into that relationship, and boom! I got dumped; for a younger woman, of course. And here I am with a contract to write yet another book on relationships. Ironically, the chapter I'm working on currently is about how to survive a breakup! I began to wonder what I really knew about the whole subject of relationships. I'd had countless conversations with my close women friends, and interviewed numerous colleagues and acquaintances, all female, regarding the feminine take on boy-meets-girl and the dream of living happily ever after. Smug in my so-called happy relationship with Jack, I thought I knew it all. After the breakup, I felt compelled to get into the heads of the male population. And my book deadline was rapidly approaching. I had to find some men in a hurry. The Personals seemed to solve that problem. Plus, there was the hope that I'd find some nice guy to replace Jack, despite it being a rebound thing.

Dolores confided that the most amusing thing she discovered was that the men she talked to simply did not seem to believe the words stated in an ad, and maybe even in conversation in general. Men seem to interpret differently. They see things through their own filters. If she were to grade them on communication skills, Dolores said most men would receive a D-minus or perhaps even an F! She read me her ad:

> *Published author seeks friend/buddy for exchange of ideas, stimulating discussions, fresh insights for book-in-progress. Let's talk over lunch.*

She received a fair amount of responses and arranged for Dutch-treat lunches; in some cases, she picked up the tab because, after all, she was picking their brains.

> Alice, you can't believe it! In almost every instance, before the lunch was over, I was invited to bed! I firmly reminded each lunch partner that I had advertised for a friend/buddy only, but they refused to believe me, saying, "Nobody advertises for just a friend. Be honest, you want a lover, right?" It was a kick in a way, because I was older than most of these guys, yet they all had the same thing in mind: sex! After my royal dumping by Jack, that was good for my ego, but honestly, Alice, can't these guys read? What happened to communication anyway? Isn't anyone paying attention to the words we say?

"It's those filters, Dolores," I reminded her. "We respond to what we think we hear, or in this case, the men responded to what they preferred to believe rather than what was actually said or stated. Or maybe it's simply wishful thinking on their part. Maybe they even think they'll get lucky. The nothing-ventured, nothing-gained approach!"

We are communicators in every area of life

We've talked a lot about personal communication here because all communication is basically between people. Of course there is communication outside of personal relationships: communication in business, at the workplace, and in virtually every aspect of our daily lives. Sometimes we're in a position to tell people what to do; other times we're in a subservient position and must take orders. We're still dealing with people. No matter who we are or what we do in life, we all are communicators and, as such, are utilizing one of the four basic forms of communication: reading, writing, speaking, and listening.

Listen and learn

Volumes could be written on the subject of listening alone. Have you ever taken a class on listening? I think not, although somewhere along the line in your life you've probably been exposed to some sort of training on the other three forms of communication: reading, writing, and speaking. They are all important, but often listening attentively with true interest in what the other person has to say can be the most necessary skill of all.

The first duty of love is to listen.

—PAUL TILLICH

Stephen R. Covey in his inspiring national best-seller, *The Seven Habits of Highly Effective People,* says, "Seek first to understand, then to be understood." If we don't listen, how can we begin to understand? Most of us, and I am a frequent offender, listen only to reply. I'm listening to what you have to say while I'm composing what I hopefully think is a helpful answer. I am hearing through my own filters. Sometimes I am not "seeking first to understand." In my defense, I must say that this is my current self-improvement project: to listen totally; to seek first to understand before replying with my so-called pearls of wisdom.

Let us all undertake to improve our communication skills. Think of how different the world would be if we were able to truly understand each other! But it all must begin on the home front. If parents could successfully communicate with their children, if teachers could communicate with their students, if we all would seek to understand those who seem troubled or act differently, perhaps such tragedies such as the Littleton, Colorado, school shooting could be avoided.

> *Oh God, help us not to despise or oppose what we do not understand.*
>
> —WILLIAM PENN

I think good communication skills begin at home when a child is barely out of the cradle. In last week's *San Francisco Chronicle,* I came across a fascinating article. The University of California at Davis Center for Child and Family Studies is teaching parents how to communicate with their infants before the toddler stage. They do this through "signing," or a series of gestures, which we normally reserve for the deaf or hearing-impaired. I quote briefly from the article:

The result, according to many child development experts, is less frustration, more understanding, and a better ability to grasp abstract concepts—and that's just for the parents. The children enjoy all of those advantages, and more.

"Babies know what they want, but they can't express it," says Dr. Ralph Berberich, a Berkeley pediatrician who has launched a baby signs program. "By having parents and caregivers gesture simple ideas to babies, they will learn to 'talk' many months before they are able to form actual words."

For more information on this interesting concept, look for the book *Baby Signs: How to Talk with Your Baby Before Your Baby Can Talk* by child-development specialists Linda Acredolo of UC Davis and Susan Goodwin of California State University, Stanislaus. Acredolo reported on some of their findings:

We looked at the core group of our original study, many who are now 9 and 10 years old. The kids who were baby signers scored significantly higher on standard IQ tests than those who didn't learn the gesturing. You can really see how things a child learns in the first couple of years of their life can have a major impact later on.

Even though we, obviously, and our children, probably, are too old to take advantage of the signing concept, it is never to late to improve our communication skills.

Were we to fully understand the reasons for other people's behavior, it would all make sense.

—SIGMUND FREUD

Now let us review some of the points brought up in this discussion of communication.

- Understand the problem before undertaking a solution. As Stephen Covey says, "Seek first to understand, then to be understood."

- Listen with empathy. Put yourself in the position of the person speaking.

- Listen with all your being: eyes, ears, and heart. Ten percent of communication is represented by the words we say; 30 percent by our sounds (tone of voice and volume); and 60 percent by our body language.

- Listen for the speaker's feeling, true meaning, emotions, and, often, plea for help. Listen without judgment or ridicule.

- Clarify your ideas before attempting to communicate in return.

- Consider any possible overtones or subtext beyond the basic content of the message.

- Go beyond being understood; strive to understand.

- Make a commitment to yourself, now, to obey Commandment VII, Communicate Effectively in All Areas of Life.

Be kind for everyone you meet is fighting a hard battle.

—PLATO

My Resolutions

In regard to Commandment VII, *Communicate Effectively in All Areas of Life,* these are my resolutions:

....

....

....

....

....

....

....

....

....

....

....

....

....

....

....

....

....

....

....

....

....

....

....

Be Tolerant and Compassionate— Develop Empathy and Forgive

Whatever you may be sure of, be sure of this—that you are dreadfully like other people.

—JAMES RUSSELL LOWELL

IF we are, in fact, dreadfully like other people, why are we so often intolerant or prejudiced? Why do we find fault with other people's culture, habits, ways of doing things—even their thoughts?

I think we've been programmed from childhood, and probably unintentionally, by those, usually parents, who cast their personal prejudices upon their children without the slightest knowledge of the harm they are doing. So we spend our early years under the false assumption that only we are the good guys, the desirable ones, and the rest of the population is inferior, lower class, or even to be feared.

My friend Paul says, "The human mind, as it develops from childhood, seems only to want to accept other humans who are almost complete mirror images. We make such a fuss over differences even if we do not express our differences directly. Why? Do we need reflections of ourselves to feel okay? It would appear so."

Paul went on to point out that people of various ethnic and cultural groups tend to gather together, and people from the same origins and ancestry like to live in proximity with one another. And, he believes, from the beginning of time, people have been apprehensive of those who are "different." I wrote an entire chapter on this phenomenon in my first book, *The Positive Thinker*. Entitled "The Law of Attraction," it discusses such popular clichés as "like attracts like" and "birds of a feather flock together" as well as other aspects of the Law of Attraction. If you've not thought about it before, ask yourself now why you live where you live, have the job you have, associate with the people that you do, and participate in certain leisure-time activities. You'll discover that in great part, it's due to the Law of Attraction.

Yes, people are drawn to certain people, places, and activities because they can relate to them and be more comfortable with them than in an alien environment. Paul summarized his thoughts on the subject by saying, "Indeed, most people seem more comfortable with boundary lines etched into the very mantling of the self. It does come, in part, from when we were in our primitive state. The safety of the cave with our own small clan was much sought after and clung to. To venture out too far, finding people who were strange in odd ways, was to court death. In short, intolerance is built on fear. And fear is a natural protection stance."

*Fear is the main source of superstition, and one
of the main sources of cruelty. To conquer fear
is the beginning of freedom.*

—BERTRAND RUSSELL

Tolerance defined

According to the *Merriam-Webster Dictionary of English Usage,* the noun "tolerance" usually means "willingness to tolerate." Yes, we must be *willing* to tolerate. The entry also mentions tolerance of viewpoints, tolerance of dissent, and the "ability to tolerate." The latter refers to a built-up acceptance by those who have addictions, such as to drugs or alcohol, or to oft-used medically prescribed substances. This chapter is concerned with one's *willingness* to tolerate, with the mind and heart, in a conscious way, rather than the *ability* to tolerate on the part of the body.

My other *Webster* defines tolerance as "sympathy or indulgence for beliefs or practices differing or conflicting with one's own." My favorite semanticist, S. I. Hayakawa, says, "Tolerant . . . approaches a neutral description in most uses. In addition to indicating a flexible attitude toward rules or standards, it can suggest approval for an open-minded reluctance to make hasty judgments or disapproval for condescending rather than equal treatment. For example: He informed his students that he could be tolerant of those who fell asleep in his class provided they didn't snore; tolerant of the attitudes and beliefs of others; tolerant of but not enthusiastic about the new teenage fads."

Tolerance is a relatively small word with several important meanings, and it carries a great deal of clout.

As stated above, the noun usually means a "willingness to tolerate." If you hope or expect to coexist peacefully with others—your family members, neighbors, coworkers, and members of your community—you must learn tolerance. You must be *willing* to tolerate. Give other people a chance. Look for their uniqueness, their good qualities; I assure you they have them.

Recently, I was walking down Lakeshore Avenue in Oakland on my usual round of errands. This is the neighborhood business area where I do my banking, go to the post office, and shop for small items like greeting cards, deli items, and produce. I'm on this street several times a week but usually pay little notice to the many others traversing the sidewalk along with me. On this particular day, I paid close attention to the people approaching me from the other direction. What a cross section of humanity! Every skin color and ethnic origin was represented; every age from infants in buggies, toddlers held by the hand, to the very elderly with their canes or walkers. There were skimpily clad teenagers with nose rings and tattoos, and well-dressed society matrons. Young boys on skateboards and businessmen hurrying to important meetings. And, as usual, there were a number of people walking their dogs. Each person, busily pursuing his or her individual goals, desires, hopes, and dreams, had a reason to be on Lakeshore Avenue, just like me. As we rushed about our daily activities, we were, for the most part, totally oblivious of each other.

I suddenly related to them, all of them, if it's possible to relate to such a scattered mixture of mankind. I thought, "We're *really* all alike! Each and every person on this street, except possibly for the infants, is a swirling mass of hopes, dreams, concerns, doubts, fears—all the emotions known to man. I am not alone," I thought with a sense of great revelation. Far from simply tolerating them, I actually felt something akin to love for them. Perhaps instead of tolerance, I was feeling compassion and empathy. The words are closely related and we'll discuss them all before this chapter ends.

On the subject of tolerance, Bob, another pen pal, wrote:

Tolerance is an interesting word. These days it seems to mean that anything is okay if it isn't done to me. I suppose there is an element of self-protection in that view, but I can't say I subscribe to it. On the other hand, the kind of intolerance that says, "If I don't like it, anybody who does is a bad person" seems rampant these days. True tolerance grows from understanding and is an element of wisdom, I think. Real tolerance is perhaps not possible without at least some empathy, another interesting word.

While I have believed in tolerance as a value since I started thinking, whenever that was, empathy has not come easily or naturally for me. My first experience of an empathetic kind occurred when I was five years old, in the summer between kindergarten and first grade. My mother had taken me to downtown Los Angeles for shopping, and then to the wholesale produce market where my father was working as a security guard. While at the market I saw a homeless man with a five-gallon can hanging from his neck by a leather strap, going from one garbage can to another salvaging edible scraps. I suppose I had never before experienced how sad and hard life could be, and I cried inconsolably. My mother, herself a very warm and empathetic person, understood, but my father thought I was behaving like a sissy, and called that poor old man a "bum."

One cannot weep for the entire world. It is be-yond human strength. One must choose.

—JEAN ANOUILH

Children often, in play with others, seem like untamed savages. It appears that civility, consideration of others, and tolerance are not inborn, but need to be taught. On the other hand, sometimes children show an uncanny empathy, tolerance, and compassion for others, as evidenced by Bob's story.

Recently, my not-yet-four-year-old grandson Campbell was listening to his father complain about the new housing developments popping up all about their rural homestead, encroaching upon their privacy. "But, Daddy," Campbell said in his adorable little voice, "everybody deserves a house and a place to live." In another conversation in which Dad was complaining again, this time about the endless rain that put the horses up to their "armpits" in mud, Campbell said, "But, Daddy, we need the rain. God makes it rain so that the flowers have water. And it makes the grass green, too." Wise words of tolerance from wee ones.

Some thoughts on compassion

Webster says compassion means to sympathize; sympathetic consciousness of other's distress together with a desire to alleviate it. Hayakawa, in comparing sympathy and compassion, says the Greek "sympathetic" has a wider, frequently more generalized, and impersonal range than the Latin "compassionate." One can be sympathetic, Hayakawa says, with a point of view, a philosophy, belief, or way of life, or feel sympathy for the hardships of a fictional character, but compassion implies a stronger and more directly personal feeling for suffering and misfortune at the individual level.

In my view, compassion is about opening one's heart to the suffering and distress of another. This can put you in a state of vulnerability, because when you open your heart, you let all of your emotional barriers down. When I read a sad story in the newspaper, or hear about a tragic event on radio or TV, I become distraught. I feel it as if it happened to me or one of my loved ones. I desperately want to help those involved, yet there is nothing I can do. When the Littleton, Colorado, shootings occurred, I would not, could not read the papers or watch the coverage of the massacre on TV for the entire week that it was a headline story. As a parent, I identified with the parents of the victims as well as of the perpetrators; I was overcome with grief for them and the young people involved. Had I followed the story closely, I would not have been able to cope with the magnitude of the tragedy and its sad aftermath. Definitely, I do not believe that our forefathers who drafted the Second Amendment granting citizens the right to keep and bear arms had it in mind that children would ever be in a position to kill other children.

More thoughts on compassion

Bob had some interesting thoughts on the subject:

Compassion, close cousin to empathy and perhaps more engaged in terms of feeling deeply about the human condition, is not easy to achieve in this age of self-absorption. Sometimes it produces unintended consequences; an example would be the military intervention in Kosovo, in which the compassionate feelings of the American people (and their intervention) have produced some fearful results. One can only hope and believe that in the end good will overcome evil. Certainly, merely resisting evil is not the way, as our best friend and perfect teacher showed in His life.

And lead us not into temptation, but deliver us from evil.

> —THE LORD'S PRAYER

Many years ago, after the Korean conflict, I talked with another military wife about her experience of compassion. I'll call my friend Margaret, and this is what she told me.

Roger, my husband, was flying missions in Korea. Our means of communication was limited, obviously, a letter here and there, or an occasional audiotape; we both had tape recorders and found the exchange of tapes a more personal way to keep in touch. Occasionally, there'd be a snapshot or two. I've always been very intuitive, and somewhere along the line, I got the notion that Roger was having a romance with the young Korean woman pictured in some of the photos. But I was young, naive, and trusting at the time, and simply couldn't believe that he would have anything to do with any woman other than me.

When Roger returned a year and a half later, I was ecstatic. He was quiet, morose, not his usual self, but I blamed the war and his combat experiences for that. A contributing factor, of course, but then I came across the box of envelopes. There were a vast number, several hundred I think. Each envelope was addressed, in the most beautiful handwriting I've ever seen, to what appeared to be a female name; Korean, of course.

We never discussed the envelopes; I think he threw them away. I do not believe he ever used a single one to write to the woman who so carefully addressed each and every one so that she would have a way to hear from and keep in touch with her American lover.

Naive I was, but as a woman I knew, *instantly knew,* the true situation. I felt a tremendous sadness and overwhelming compassion, and still do to this day, for the young woman, who lived so far away, in another world really, who was and may still be pining for my Roger, hopelessly waiting in vain to hear from him. To this day, I cannot begin to think of ever again attending the opera *Madame Butterfly.* The story has become far too personal for me. Even thinking of it causes me to dissolve in tears, as I totally empathize with the plight of the tragic young heroine.

Margaret concluded: "War is cruel, and so are many men."

> *It is not merely cruelty that leads men to love war, it is excitement.*
>
> —HENRY WARD BEECHER

Margaret told me that for years after this episode, and even though they never discussed it, she judged Roger. She felt deep compassion for the young woman in Korea, perhaps because as a woman imagining herself in the Korean woman's place, she assumed Roger to be at fault. She thought, as Beecher stated, that he was looking for excitement. He alone caused the situation; it was all his fault, she determined. As time went by, Margaret was able to feel compassion for both of the young lovers; finally allowing the thought to enter her mind that these things just happen, and she permitted her negative judgments against Roger to dissipate.

> *How can we venture to judge others when we know so well how ill-equipped they are for judging us?*
>
> —COMTESSE DIANA

Empathy

Empathy, according to the *Dictionary of Problem Words and Expressions,* refers to actual identification with the thoughts and feelings of someone else or to a sharing through vicarious experiences with the attitudes and emotions of another.

The first time I became totally acquainted and saturated with the word was when I attended a high-powered sales seminar conducted by an electrifying speaker who made a tremendous impact on me. It was one of the first of many such seminars that I attended while in the field of sales, but the great impression this one made had to do with the constant use of the word "empathy." In fact, as a handout, each of those attending was given a piece of cardboard about 18 by 2½ inches high with the word EMPATHY emblazoned on the front in large block letters. The cardboard was constructed in such a way that by folding, it could made into a standing sign; it was designed to sit on one's desk to be observed and absorbed during one's entire time in the office. The idea, of course, was for us, as salespeople, to empathize with our present and potential clients; to, as the definition above states, actually identify with the thoughts and feelings as well as the attitudes and emotions of the client. Since then, as I empathized my way to become top biller and head of the department with true sincerity, empathy has been one of my favorite words.

Empathizing with our clients, as well as friends, neighbors, and others in our personal circle, is one thing, but what about the times when the need to empathize hits much closer to our hearts and homes? Of course we empathize when our loved ones are sad, when they have problems and suffer setbacks, both major and minor. But can we truly empathize when we, personally, are the ones hurt by those closest and dearest to us? I am coping with this situation as I write.

My dearest friend, live-in companion of twenty years, and, I thought, life partner, who conducts tours in Southeast Asia, recently informed me that he is in love with a woman from that area who is almost half my age. Madly, passionately, completely, and hopelessly in love. The situation is complicated by the fact that the woman is married, unhappily, to another man. As is often the case in Third World countries, her husband had, without divorce, taken on a second wife who produced his much-wanted son. Since the woman is the first wife and considered a possession, the husband refuses to divorce her and, not only that, has threatened to kill her if she files for divorce or continues to communicate in any way with my friend. She has become a virtual prisoner in her home and on the job; all women in Vietnam work, in fact, they are the backbone of the country's workforce.

During most of my waking hours, while in a personal state of emotional devastation myself, I am faced with consoling my former lover, who is beside himself with worry and concern over his new beloved, whom he hopes to marry if the monumental problems can be overcome. Does this take compassion and empathy, or what? Most of the time I cope; occasionally I go off the deep end.

This is what I call a sticky wicket, a no-win situation of the first order. In the meantime, and while new information about the circumstances and hopeful plans of the lovers are revealed to me daily, my friend, who now bears the title "roommate," still resides in my home. Soap-opera stuff. Almost the *Madame Butterfly* situation Margaret replayed. Perhaps this time around, the more recent production of *Miss Saigon* is more literally relevant.

Talk about the need for tolerance, compassion, empathy, and forgiveness! I am drenched in it. How did this ever happen to me, I wonder?

> *A woman's life can really be a succession of lives, each revolving around some emotionally compelling situation or challenge.*

—WALLIS SIMPSON, Duchess of Windsor

I know life is supposed to be a series of lessons that, once learned, allow one to progress. But how many times must I take the same course? I've been there, done that, I tell God. "Class remains in session, Alice," He replies. "You still have much more to learn."

Was I, am I, angry with the situation that was handed to me and seems outside of my control? Yes, absolutely. But that only adds to the insomnia and other ills connected with anger, and there are many.

> *Heaven hath no rage like love to hatred turned,*
> *Nor hell a fury like a woman scorned.*

—WILLIAM CONGREVE

What is the answer? Although I blame my friend and his Asian love because they allowed the situation to occur knowing the obstacles, while totally ignoring the feelings of others involved, I feel tremendous compassion for all of us. So, with all of my creative abilities, I constantly offer solutions to my friend, hoping one will fit the complex intricacies of the situation. The latest idea, which was his, not mine, is to mount a campaign to assist all females in the woman's country to overcome male domination and achieve equal rights. I believe in finding one's life purpose and living it, and perhaps this is his.

One's life has value so long as one attributes value to the life of others, by means of love, friendship, indignation and compassion.

—SIMONE DE BEAUVOIR

In the meantime, I must go forward and reconstruct my life. Not easy in the twilight of one's years. But I am persevering, and despite the tears, there are many hilarious moments! I am dating new men—an experience that shall be the focus of my next book. You will be amused, I assure you! For example, can you image having a new date arrive to pick you up for dinner only to have your old friend and lover, now "roommate," greet him at the door? This takes tolerance—and a great sense of humor!

Ah, but in the long run, it all comes down to forgiveness. I've written much about forgiveness in previous books and have to come to realize that, ultimately, forgiveness is the only solution to many of life's unforgivable situations.

When I allow myself to dwell on my anger, the deep hurt, and my resentments brought on by this betrayal, I become drained and can hardly function. If I allow myself to cry, even though they say crying is cathartic, I become a virtual basket case. So I resist victimhood. Every time I realize that my thoughts are leading to the devastating pit-of-the-stomach sadness that inevitably precedes the terror, anxiety attack, and ultimate loss of control that I fear above all, I cry, *"Stop!"* Sometimes it takes more than one "Stop!" but the method does work for me. It clears my mind and forces me to understand that my errant thoughts are doing this to me. Because the situation will not change; I must change my thoughts.

And I must forgive. I must forgive myself for my anger and occasional blowups over the situation. I must forgive my friend and his beloved because, as Margaret learned, sometimes these things just happen. And I must understand that there is a lesson for me, and the others involved, in all of this. There is an opportunity for growth in every lesson, and I must focus on that. And I must focus on the new and brighter future that is sure to come. Definitely, I'll be a far wiser woman thanks to this experience. As a bonus, I'll retrieve the energy, pride, and self-esteem so badly damaged by the hurt, humiliation, and pain brought on by the situation.

A plea for forgiveness

Here's another forgiveness story of a sort, recently relayed to me by a friend of many years. Rosalynn married her high-school sweetheart during the war, as did many of us. I'm referring to World War II, of course. After Sam got out of the service, they settled down in his hometown, where he started his own business. Rosalynn filled the role of wife, mother, and homemaker perfectly. But as the years went by and the business succeeded, Rosalynn felt their standard of living did not keep pace. She felt that in their social circle, they were not quite keeping up with the Joneses. She pressed Sam for the usual outward displays of affluence: a better car, a bigger house, more jewelry, and furs. Sam, being a conservative yet indulgent man, allowed Rosalynn most of her wishes, but stalled on the issue of a bigger, grander house. He felt their present home was more than adequate for their family, and resisted her pleas and arguments for the elegant edifice upon which her heart was set.

The whole thing became such a heated issue that Rosalynn threatened to leave Sam. In fact, she thought a visit to her cousin in another state might show Sam how much he'd miss her if she left, and she took off for an indefinite stay with the cousin. By now, the children were in college, so she was not deserting her duties, only teaching Sam a lesson.

Sam missed Rosalynn dreadfully from day one. He felt so bad physically that he finally went to the doctor, something he'd never permitted himself to do previously because the business always came first; certainly before worrying about one's health or physical condition. But he had waited too long; Sam was diagnosed with an incurable, terminal disease and given a limited time to live.

Of course, Rosalynn rushed back home to nurse Sam in his last months. For many reasons, this was not the time to be an absent wife. She did not forget about the house issue, nor did Sam, evidently. On his deathbed, when he could barely speak, he whispered in a halting voice, "Rosalynn, my dear wife, I love you so. I appreciate your coming back to care for me these past months. Will you, can you in your heart forgive me for denying you the house of your dreams? It would mean so very much to me. Please, please forgive me." Rosalynn answered with one word: "No." Sam closed his eyes and died before the day was over.

I listened to this story with eyes wide and mouth open. Was that the end of the story? "Yes," Rosalynn said, laughing proudly. "I said 'No!' And I said it emphatically! I guess he got the message! Forgive? You've got to be kidding!"

> *Ultimately, there is nothing to forgive, because there is nothing to judge and no one to blame.*
>
> —WAYNE DYER

But it wasn't the end of the story. Sam was heavily insured and one of his policies bought Rosalynn the house of her dreams. Then the successful business Sam started and worked at so diligently sold for a substantial sum, thereby providing Rosalynn a lifetime of worry-free luxury.

Although she is adamant that she will never forgive him, perhaps Rosalynn could have shown some compassion for Sam, who, she concedes, was obviously sincere in his deathbed plea for forgiveness. She might have heeded the advice of John F. Kennedy, who said, "Forgive but never forget."

In politics, as in affairs of state, that philosophy probably holds true. But in human relations, I beg to differ with President Kennedy. If you forgive, *truly* forgive, that should be it. You must consider the matter done with, finished forever. I do not believe that one should, as Kennedy said, "never forget." That just keeps the wound brought on by the initial action festering. If you forgive, forget. Do not continue to harbor thoughts about the matter. Those thoughts are internally destructive, and you and you alone are the one being destroyed, not the other party.

Forgiveness has vast benefits. As I said in a previous book, "Forgiveness is freeing and liberating. It can give us peace. Without it we can become bitter, angry, and full of pain—if we aren't already—and withdrawn. Others can become hostile and aggressive, along with the aforementioned adjectives, without the cleansing aspects of forgiveness. The opposite of forgiveness is hatred, and hatred is a tremendous burden."

If you truly cannot forgive, and many actions are so despicable that one, in all honesty, cannot be expected to forgive, then I suggest you forget. Put it out of your mind. Let it go. Free yourself from the shackles in which lack of forgiveness enslaves you. If you refuse to forgive—or to forget—or to let it go, you will be forever tied to your adversary. Just as it takes two to tango, according to cosmic law, it takes two to make a prisoner; the prisoner and his jailer. Therefore, unless you set the hated person free, you will remain as attached to him cosmically as if you were handcuffed to each other. Why allow yourself to be emotionally attached to someone you despise or dislike?

Forgive. If you can't forgive, forget. If you can't forget, simply let it go. Do it for yourself, not the other person. Because if you don't, you will be the one who suffers, mentally, physically, and spiritually, while your adversary goes free.

Blame keeps wounds open. Only forgiveness heals.

—WILLA CATHER

Ultimate forgiveness

California, where I live, is a death-penalty state. And public-opinion polls show that three in four Californians support the death penalty, as does our governor. When a heinous crime, such as murder, is committed, most people clamor for justice, demanding "an eye for an eye." And when a convicted murderer is about to be executed, there is much in the press about the need for retaliation and closure, the notion being that execution will bring closure, or a measure of peace, to the families of the victims.

For some, execution of the perpetrator, after years of waiting, is sweet and a time for celebration. For others, forgiveness is the better way. One mother, mourning the death of her nineteen-year-old daughter at the hands of a drifter, credits a spiritual transformation that inspired her to forgiveness. "It was an epiphany," she recalled. "A voice came to me and said, 'You must forgive him, and let him know.'"

This woman is now an active member of Murder Victims for Reconciliation, a nationwide group of two thousand people who have lost relatives to murder but are still against the death penalty. She wrote to her daughter's murderer and eventually went into San Quentin Prison to meet him. According to the *San Francisco Chronicle,* this is what she saw: "I expected to see a room full of monsters, and what I saw was a room full of ordinary men. They were very quiet, intelligent and polite, being visited by their wives, mothers and children. All it took for me was to meet this man to see how wrong the death penalty is." This woman's peace of mind was found through forgiveness.

To want to avenge a loved one's death may be human nature. "It's very common," said Dr. Paul Berg, an Oakland, California, psychologist in the pages of the *San Francisco Examiner*. "In some people it seems to last forever. It's not a healthy reaction. No one can thrive on being pissed off all the time."

Pat Bane, past president of Murder Victims' Families for Reconciliation, said, "You spend 10 years hating someone, then you wake up the next morning, and he's dead"—i.e., executed. What do you do with that hatred? They haven't healed because that grief has been put on hold, waiting for some magic bullet to end it all."

Here's another story of supreme forgiveness, reported in the Sunday *San Francisco Examiner*. Brooks Douglass, an Oklahoma state senator, when on a tour of his state's prison system, visited the man who savagely killed his family and raped his sister twenty years ago. While sitting across a glass divide from the murderer, Douglass had an out-of-body experience. Later, as he got up to leave, he said to the inmate, "I forgive you." "All of a sudden, it felt like it was poison pouring out of the bottom of my feet. It was one of the most physical sensations I've ever had, like someone took a clamp off my chest. I felt like I could breathe again for the first time in 15 years." Douglass says he still supports the death penalty in particularly vicious and cruel cases. To him, "it is a matter for the criminal justice system, while forgiveness is the answer to coping at the emotional and personal level."

Forgive, and ye shall be forgiven.

—LUKE 6:37

Let me summarize the message in this Commandment by saying:

• *Be tolerant* by being willing to tolerate.

- *Be compassionate* by having a sympathetic consciousness of another's distress.

- *Develop empathy* by identifying with the thoughts and feelings of someone else or, by sharing, through vicarious experience, the attitudes and emotions of another.

- *Forgive* by freeing yourself and pardoning with compassion.

Resolve to be tender with the young, compassionate with the aged, sympathetic with the striving, and tolerant with the weak and the wrong. Sometime in life you will have been all of these.

—LLOYD SHEARER

My Resolutions

In regard to Commandment VIII, *Be Tolerant and Compassionate—Develop Empathy and Forgive,* these are my resolutions:

....
....
....
....
....
....
....
....
....
....
....
....
....
....
....
....
....
....
....
....
....

Love One Another

A new commandment I give unto you, that you love one another.

—JOHN 13:34

LOVE! A four-letter word with far more impact than the many others that fall into that category. We bandy the word "love" about as if it were a tennis or a Ping-Ping ball, giving it many diverse meanings. "I love my wife, but I also love pizza . . . bowling . . . sports on TV." "I love my children . . . my country . . . my pickup truck . . . my dog/cat." "I love weekends . . . days in the country . . . hiking in the hills . . . soaking in the sun." "I love reading . . . movies . . . popcorn and ice cream." One could go through the alphabet, from A to Z, reciting the many things one loves.

But is love the proper word? Perhaps we mean "like." We are supposed to love our spouses and children, but should our love for pizza, bowling, and sports have the same intensity? Perhaps what we really mean is that we *love* our spouse and kids because we have great affection and deep emotional feelings for them, but that we *like* the many other items on our list.

Then there are other connotations of the word love.

You can be *in* love ... *make* love ... and *become* love-sick. You can *do* something for love ... *send* love ... *have* a love affair ... or *tie* a love knot. You can *write* love letters ... *build* a love nest ... or *prepare* a love potion. Or, you can say, *"Not for love or money* will I do so and so." As you can readily see, love is a frequently used, and often misused, word.

Love can take many forms. A mother loves her child; a man feels passionate love for his sweetheart; you may have a fond and loving attachment for your pet. The word can denote the deep emotion a person feels for some*one* ... for some*thing,* such as love of country ... or for a higher entity, such as love of God. Love is a word that binds by ties of heart or mind. Let us reserve love for important relationships and not trivialize it by associating it with other areas or occasions.

It's love that makes the world go round!

—W. S. GILBERT

But our commandment states that we must *love one another.* If we can barely tolerate one another generally, how can we *love* one another? For some illumination on the subject, I turned to I Corinthians 13:1–13.

And now I will show you the best way of all.

I may speak in different languages of men or even angels. But if I do not have love, then I am only a noisy bell or a ringing cymbal. I may have the gift of prophesy, I may understand all the secret things of God and all knowledge; and I may have faith so great that I can move mountains. But even with all

these things, if I do not have love, then I am nothing.
I may give everything I have to feed the poor. And
I may even give my body as an offering to be burned.
But I gain nothing by doing these things if I do not
have love.

Love is patient and kind. Love is not jealous, it
does not brag, and it is not proud. Love is not rude,
it is not selfish, and does not become angry easily.
Love does not remember wrongs done against it.
Love is not happy with evil, but is happy with the
truth. Love patiently accepts all things. It always
trusts, always hopes, and always continues strong.

Love never ends. There are gifts of prophesy, but
they will be ended. There are gifts of speaking in
different languages, but those gifts will end. There is
the gift of knowledge, but it will be ended. These
things will end, because this knowledge and these
prophecies we have are not complete. But when per-
fection comes, the things that are not complete will
end. When I was a child, I talked like a child; I
thought like a child; I made plans like a child. When
I became a man, I stopped those childish ways. It is
the same with us. Now we see as if we are looking
into a dark mirror. But at that time, in the future, we
shall see clearly. Now I know only a part. But at that
time I will know fully, as God has known me. So
these three things continue forever: faith, hope and
love. And the greatest of these is love.

*Love is all we have, the only way that each can
help the other.*

—EURIPIDES

Yes, let us help one another. Annette Martin, who schedules on-air guests for Power Talk Radio, John St. Augustine's dynamite morning positive-thinking radio program, heard daily on WDBC in Escanaba, Michigan, related this personal story of help she received from an unknown source:

It was the summer of '98 when I heard John St. Augustine talk for the first time. Afterward, I wanted so much to work with him. But it wasn't until January of '99 when, due to losing a telephone number given to me by a counselor at the local hospital, I was instead given the number to The Link, a community information center in which John is active, that I was again connected to him.

While at The Link, John overheard me tell someone about having $200 in bills that had to be paid by that Friday, three days away. I had $150, but had no idea where the other $50 would come from. John told me to take $10 and give it to someone I didn't know, but who I felt needed it worse than I did. I thought he was nuts! That meant I would need $60 more, not just $50. John added that he would guarantee the $50 for me; if I did not receive it by Friday, he would give it to me personally.

I took $10 and went to St. Vincent de Paul looking for an appropriate recipient, but had no luck. Later, I went to my Alanon meeting and received the same response there as I had gotten at The Link. The next day, I tried St. Vincent de Paul again. Again, no luck. I walked around our plaza and shopping center; still no appropriate recipient. Later, I ended up spending the $10 on groceries for my daughter and myself.

The following day, my paycheck turned out to be $40 more than I expected. Later that same day, I received an anonymous letter with $5 enclosed and a note saying, "A little something to help a little." Then, on Friday, I received an envelope that had been dropped off for me. In it was $50.

The original $10 that I had every intention of giving away (and since then I have) turned into $105 by Friday. Thank you, John, for restoring my belief in a Higher Power. I won't lose sight of Him again.

Was the receipt of the needed money an anonymous expression of love from Annette's friends, or was it a gift from a Higher Power? Or both?

The ultimate lesson all of us have to learn is unconditional love, which includes not only others, but ourselves as well.

—ELISABETH KÜBLER-ROSS

Yes, we must love others, but we must also learn to love ourselves. As with most things, love begins at home. If we do not have love in our hearts and minds, we cannot express love. We must find love within and nurture it; only then will it materialize in our lives; only then will we have the gift of love to give to others. As stated in I Corinthians, "If I do not have love, I am nothing."

> *One must love oneself with a wholesome and*
> *healthy love, so that one can bear to be with*
> *oneself and need not roam.*
>
> —FRIEDRICH NIETZSCHE

What can we do to turn the Corinthians statement from the negative, "If I do not have love, then I am nothing," to the positive, "If I have love, then I am everything"? In other words, how can we share love after we have mastered the difficult task of loving ourselves?

One of my favorite ways is to send out anonymous "love messages." These gifts of love are, as I said, anonymous, and they should be sent to those we don't know. I like to do this when I'm on a busy bus or a subway train. For me, public transportation is more conducive for love thoughts than driving a car. While driving, I must totally concentrate on the road and I have no time for musing about my fellow travelers who could undoubtedly use a bit of love to assuage their road rage. On the other hand, while on a bus or train, I can sit and peruse those who are trapped, along with me, in a lackluster vehicle we may prefer not to inhabit.

I then pick out someone who looks lonely, tired, or worried. Mentally, I direct a message to him or her that goes something like this: "You are a fine person. Someone cares for you. Everything will be all right." Amazingly, the person usually comes to attention and looks around expectantly. Somehow, telepathically or psychically, they received the message. If my trip takes thirty or forty minutes, I can send out many messages to harried commuters. My hope is that the recipients feel uplifted; I know I feel uplifted by my secret communications.

The giving of love is an education in itself.
—ELEANOR ROOSEVELT

My good friend Mary offers her personal way of loving others:

Pray daily. Just a few prayers when you're driving. It's amazing how many things and/or people you can remember in a short time. I drive in from Walnut Creek every morning, which takes about thirty minutes, and I find this is a great time to thank God for blessings and also remember people that I want to pray for.

A single grateful thought raised to heaven is the most perfect prayer.

—GOTTHOLD EPHRAIM

The man who waved

For years, a man stood on a Berkeley street corner for eight hours every day, rain or shine, and waved to commuters and neighborhood regulars as they drove by. When asked why he did it, he replied, "It makes me feel good." And it made the people he waved at feel good, too. Many made it a habit to go by the man's corner daily to wave and be waved at. After twenty years, the man announced he was retiring; to him, waving at his countless unknown friends had become a full-time job. There was an enormous celebration to mark the elderly man's retirement, and his story made the front pages of many local and major California newspapers. I don't know what he is doing now, but I'm sure he has many, many happy memories of his time spent sharing love with others.

The man who smiled at everyone

San Francisco had a character named Ira Carter whose profession seemed to be hanging out on the corner of Twenty-sixth and Mission in front of the Tip Top Inn. With the two dogs that were always with him, Ira was a fixture Everyone knew him; he always had a smile and kind word for people on their way to and from work. He never asked anyone for anything except possibly for a smile in return when he'd call out, "Hey, Baby" or "Good morning. Are you having any fun?" Most people didn't reply, this is The City, after all, and they knew not to speak to strangers. Ira is gone now, and everyone misses him. "He was always so happy," someone said, "and he made us happy, too." In his memory, the Tip Top mounted a poem about him on the outside wall. Ira wasn't famous, but he left an indelible mark on the city known as San Francisco.

I'm not suggesting that you stand on a street corner and wave at passersby as did the man in Berkeley, or that you call out greetings to the passing parade in your city. But I am suggesting that you do what you can daily to lift the spirits of those with whom you come in contact.

The man who always had a kind word

Charlie sold newspapers from a tiny hole-in-the-wall stall next to the Grand Lake Theater in Oakland. He,

too, was a fixture. If you didn't have home delivery of
your newspaper, you picked one up from Charlie. Or if
you wanted to keep up with what was happening back
home, you ordered your out-of-town papers from Charlie. Charlie, like Ira, always had a kind word for everyone who entered his crowded shop. Occasionally, I'd
stop by to pick up a copy of the Sunday *New York Times*
and Charlie would invariably have a compliment for me.
"You look so pretty today, Miss Alice." When Charlie
died, a pall descended upon the entire neighborhood. He
had touched so many lives with his smiles and sincere
compliments. I still think of him every time I walk past
the shop he tended so carefully for over thirty-five years.

I can live for two months on a good compliment.

—MARK TWAIN

Telephone and other kindness stories

Around the Christmas holiday last year, I answered
the ringing phone with my usual hello. The caller instantly realized that she had reached a wrong number,
and instead of curtly stating, "Oops, wrong number," she
said, "I'm terribly sorry to have reached you in error.
God bless you. And have a very merry Christmas!" I
was pleasantly taken aback. In my entire life, no one
had ever before wished me God's blessing upon finding
I was not the party they expected to contact. How much
more cordial and civilized than the all-too-often slam-
in-the-ear of the receiver.

Another telephone story: Many years ago I was connected with a wrong number. The woman on the other

end was obviously elderly and a bit hard-of-hearing. I spoke with her for a few minutes, and before she hung up, she said, "Thank you so much for talking with me. I so seldom have calls, it was a pleasure to talk to someone, if only for a moment."

No act of kindness, no matter how small, is ever wasted.

—AESOP

We've all heard about the occasional stranger who, when paying his bridge toll, will pay for the car behind him as a gesture of goodwill. My friend Fern was the recipient of an anonymous driver's generosity recently. She was both flabbergasted and elated, and called to tell me of the unexpected act of kindness the minute she arrived home. And she wrote a letter to the editor of the *San Francisco Chronicle* to publicly thank the man because she was unable to catch up with him on the bridge to signal her thanks.

Pennies—sort of—from heaven

And here's another story of a stranger's kindness. When the rate for regular postal service went up from thirty-two to thirty-three cents, we all needed a stock of one-cent stamps to go along with the thirty-two-cent stamps we had on hand. Almost immediately my post office ran out of one-cent stamps, which was noted on a sign posted outside of the local branch. People were frustrated; how to pay their bills and deal with correspondence without adequate postage on their mail?

Finally, when the post office did receive a supply of the needed one-cent stamps, the line waiting to buy them extended out of the building and down the street.

My local branch is in a narrow building sandwiched between mom-and-pop businesses. The main area where the clerks are on duty is extremely small and badly ventilated. It is easy to become not only uncomfortable, but claustrophobic while crammed in this structure, and with only two clerks on duty, those waiting in line often become angry and hostile.

That was the case on the day I was waiting in line to mail off some books and, hopefully, to buy some one-cent stamps. A woman at the head of the line bought a large quantity of the sought-after stamps, and walking down the line of those waiting, she handed them out freely to those who were in line for the stamps only. She refused payment, saying it was her gift. At a a penny each, if she gave away twenty or thirty stamps to each person, it was no big deal, money-wise. But what a big deal it was to those accepting the stamps! It allowed them to immediately exit the suffocating post office and continue their daily business. It's amazing what a big impact this small kindness had on the crowd.

God loveth a cheerful giver.

—II CORINTHIANS 9:7

An international act of love

Here's the story of a gift of kindness that had a larger impact. My friend Hans, as I've said, conducts tours in Vietnam. A friend of his, Tom Beach, had been to Victnam on an earlier trip, and he told Hans of the desperate need for medical supplies, especially antibiotics, in a particular children's hospital. Prior to his scheduled trip, Hans contacted local doctors, hospitals, and pharmacies here to see if they had medications that they would consider donating to the children's hospital in Vietnam. Hans planned to collect donations and personally transport them to Vietnam and deliver them to the hospital. He was deluged with donations, many from doctors and pharmacists who had served in Vietnam during the war. Most offered comments like "It's my pleasure to help in some small way. It's the least I can do after what we did to them." One of the Vietnamese men who was coordinating the operation from that country sent this e-mail to Hans prior to his departure:

Dear Hans:

I'm very happy to learn that your people & you want to drop off some medical supplies for Bong Son hospital for my country, Vietnam. That's a kindness of yours. I must immediately reply on your needs.

Hans, I was emotional last time when Tom Beach gave some Asperins, Medicines & money to the poor. The local people they did not understand why an American treat them so well. Children thanked Tom gently. I recalled Tom Beach also cried.

I appreciate you very much for asking me that inquiry. I will do whatever for my country, my people. If I am a Premier, you are free to visit Vietnam without Visa!

OK! Hung is always one of your good friend in Vietnam. If you have any requests, pls email to me.

> *Best regards,*
> *Hung*

A very sincere message from someone who appreciated Hans's act of love for innocent children in a country that was once our enemy.

Wherever the art of medicine is loved, there is also the love of humanity.

> —HIPPOCRATES

A loving promise

Oral Lee Brown is an Oakland real-estate agent. She is also known as "Mama" to a class of students from Brookfield Elementary School that she adopted in 1987. In the twelve years since then, she has served as a mentor, a friend, a helping hand, and an inspiration to each and every one of these impoverished students from the ghetto. Now she is ready to make good on her pledge to pay for their college educations. Nineteen of the original twenty-three students from the first-grade class she adopted are now graduating from high school and have been accepted at such colleges as San Francisco State, Georgia Tech, Clark University, and Merritt College.

When Miss Brown, as she's also called, stood in front of the class of first-graders so long ago, she looked into their small faces and told them, "I am not here to take the place of your parents, I am here to try to help you be the best person you can be."

Every year Oral Lee Brown put $10,000 into a trust fund for the children. The money came from the commissions she made selling homes in a working-class section of Oakland. The fund will help pay for tuition and housing for her "babies," as she calls them. Miss Brown is not affluent; on the contrary, she lives in the same struggling community as do her "children." She simply wanted to help kids who, like herself, have not had it easy. Back in '87, she told the principal of the school she selected, "I want to adopt a class. I want the kids no one expects to go anywhere in life." Her kids were the lucky ones.

But Miss Brown was not just a benefactor, she was a hands-on "mama." She was personally on hand and on call almost daily as she guided her kids through elementary, middle, and high school. She bought some of the children shoes when they needed them. She fed them when there was no food in their homes. Every year there were Christmas presents. And she took them on outings and trips. Some days, between her business and the children, Oral was plain worn-out. Overall, it was much harder than she ever envisioned, but the rewards have exceeded her highest expectations. For Mother of This or Any Year, I vote for Oral Lee Brown!

In fact, Oral Lee Brown has been named a national education hero. She is among ten people in the country who did something so remarkable that U.S. Education Secretary Richard Riley plans to honor her with a John Stanford Education Hero Award. She will be Secretary Riley's guest at a ceremony at the Doyle Hotel in Washington, D.C., to honor the winners.

> *Train up a child in the way he should go: and*
> *when he is old, he will not depart from it.*
>
> —PROVERBS 22:6

A gift of love and life

Glen and Dick were friends. Not just friends, but good friends. Still, is friendship enough when it comes to donating a kidney? The statistics are a hundred to one against. As a rule, people don't donate a vital organ to anyone but a close relative.

But Glen gave his kidney to his friend Dick. Glen says it's inevitable that each of us must come to the aid of another to sustain the human race. "If you have good faith and believe in God and believe in medicine, you can save people a lot of pain."

None of Dick's family members was a medical match for the transplant, not even his fraternal twin. Surprisingly, Glen was. After the surgery, Dick, looking fit, said he was "numb" with the enormity of Glen's gift. "It is hard to believe he did this for me and my family," he said. "But Glen is the kind of guy who is just a giver, and I think he got satisfaction from giving the gift of life."

> *It is one of the most beautiful compensations of*
> *life that no man can sincerely try to help an-*
> *other without helping himself.*
>
> —RALPH WALDO EMERSON

Love is most often thought of in terms of romantic love; a man and a woman walking off into the sunset, hand in hand, living happily ever after. But what does one do when things go awry? John was happily married, or so he thought. And then one day his wife of seventeen years left him with no explanation. It was a tough year for John, but he finally got his act together. As a celebration of that, he was encouraged to present his thoughts at a reading given to the social group of the church in which he is active. John's presentation was entitled "Hello/Goodbye," and he sent it to me so that I might share it with you.

HELLO/GOODBYE
by John Gill Wright

Hello, Pretty Lady
    Hello to seventeen years of joyous love, of hugs and kisses many times a day,
      to daytime sharings and nighttime cuddles;
      to the joys of a beautiful, wonderful, exciting daughter;
      to two beautiful homes and the good life;
      to opera, culture, and travel all over the world; and the deep
      the deep, profound joy of a perfect love match.

Goodbye, wife
    Suddenly. With clues seen only in retrospect.

Hello, lawyers
    "I represent your wife—please see the attached summons—"

Goodbye, sleep
    What did I do?

What can I do?
If I can just get the right words on that letter—
Why???

Hello, kitty

    At long last, a kitty! Always wanted; always begged for; always vetoed.

    But now he's here, to slow a daughter's tears. A big hole to fill—for such a small kitty.

Goodbye, stuff

    Locks not changed; accounts not closed; hope for normalcy; don't make waves. She will be back; we will talk; this can be fixed; don't close any doors.

    Closets empty; more than that—
No word.

Hello, housework

    Cooking. Cleaning up. Laundry. Water plants (must look good when she comes back). Shopping. Picking things up from where they were dropped and putting them where they're supposed to be (for when she comes back to talk).

    Negotiate new chores with daughter. Renegotiate.

    Hello, cleaning lady!

Goodbye, Tahoe

    Twelve years of work. New kitchen, bathroom, everything. To enjoy friends and family. Never happened; my Tahoe life, my dreams of friends and children and grandchildren enjoying the lake—all gone!

Hello, daughters

Daddy and daughter go shopping for food; shop for clothes; shop for CDs and guitar strings. Go everywhere for lessons! All alone to deal with the new hormones. Scary!

Her daughter remains my daughter. A welcome gift.

Older daughters become family again; I have grandchildren!

Goodbye, Grandma

Her daughter can do no wrong; therefore I am the devil. I was her son.

Hello, mirror

What did I do? No answers. Not like the men on Dr. Laura; didn't cheat, didn't drink, didn't abuse, didn't ignore. Even left the toilet seat down!

Goodbye, pain and sadness

After time, the dust settles. I have survived— and I'm okay.

Hello, world

Renewed family ties bring joy all around. I love my daughters and am so proud of them. The stock market has been good; I can give back to help others. Have a little time to say hello to new lady friends, too!

The old must make way for the new!

I'm happy to report that John is now doing very well, thank you!

> *Self-love is not only necessary and good, it is a*
> *prerequisite for loving others.*
>
> —ROLLO MAY

A recipe for renewed love

A letter to "Dear Abby" from "Happy Again in San Diego" also addressed the problem of a shaky marriage. This is Happy Again's letter:

> *My marriage was in need of repair. My husband and I had been fighting a lot. He told me that if I didn't like it, I could pack my things and go. I cried myself to sleep for nights on end.*
>
> *One night I couldn't sleep because I was so upset with him. All I could think about were all the things that bugged me about him. I knew that if I didn't banish these negative thoughts from my mind, it would be a long time before I fell asleep. I decided to think, instead, of all the things that I loved about him. I wrote them down on a piece of paper, put it in an envelope, and placed it in his briefcase.*
>
> *The next morning, he called me from work to tell me how much he loved me. When he came home that evening, he put my "list" in a frame and hung it on the wall. We hardly ever fight anymore. I get love notes weekly and kisses daily.*
>
> *I thought some of your readers might like to try this recipe for renewed love.*

As a committed letter writer, I hardly endorse this approach. Try it. And for those who love love, I submit what I consider the most beautiful love letter ever written:

Major Ballou's letter home

A week before the Battle of Bull Run, Sullivan Ballou, a major in the 2nd Rhode Island Volunteers, wrote home to his wife in Smithfield:

July 14, 1861
Washington, D.C.

Dear Sarah:
   The indications are very strong that we shall move in a few days, perhaps tomorrow. And lest I should not be able to write to you again, I feel impelled to write a few lines that may fall under your eyes when I am no more.
   I have no misgivings about or lack of confidence in the cause in which I am engaged, and my courage does not halt or falter. I know how American civilization now leans on the triumph of the government and how great a debt we owe to those who went before us through the blood and suffering of the Revolution. And I am willing, perfectly willing to lay down all my joys in this life to help maintain this government and to pay that debt.
   Sarah, my love for you is deathless. It seems to bind me with mighty cables that nothing but Omnipotence can break. And yet my love of country comes over me like a strong wind and bears me

irresistibly, with all these chains, to the battlefield.

The memory of all the blissful moments I have enjoyed with you come crowding over me, and I feel most deeply grateful to God and you that I have enjoyed them so long. And how hard it is for me to give them up and burn to ashes the hopes of future years when, God willing, we might still have lived and loved together and seen our boys grown up to honorable manhood around us.

If I do not return, my dear Sarah, never forget how much I loved you, nor that when my last breath escapes me on the battlefield, it will whisper your name. Forgive my many faults and the many pains I have caused you. How thoughtless, how foolish I have sometimes been.

But, oh Sarah. If the dead can come back to this earth and flit unseen around those they love, I shall always be with you in the brightest day and in the darkest night. Always. Always.

And when the soft breeze fans your cheek, it shall be my breath; or the cool air your throbbing temple, it shall be my spirit passing by. Sarah, do not mourn me dead: Think I am gone and wait for me, for we shall meet again.

Sullivan Ballou was killed a week later at the first Battle of Bull Run.

A gift of love

This past week a tragic accident took the lives of three people here in the Bay Area, two men and a twelve-year-old boy, returning from a weekend retreat sponsored by a local church. What was supposed to be a weekend of fellowship and fun ended abruptly when a tire blew out on a van driving thirteen of the church-goers home.

José, the twelve-year-old boy, gave this poem to his mother the week before the accident, along with a hand-made box. Made of pastel-colored paper, the box came with this handwritten poem describing how he is always thinking of her and how the box was filled with love. Entitled "The Gift of Love," the poem was translated from the Spanish by David Corrales, a volunteer pastor whose father is the senior pastor at the church.

This is a gift, a very special gift.
It's one that you will never see,
And that is the reason why it is so special.
It is only for you from me.
When you feel alone or when you feel sad, all you
    have to do
is take the gift and know that I am thinking about
    you,
but never open it.
Please leave the ribbon tied.
Only have the box next to you.
It is filled with love.

Can you imagine how Sarah Ballou felt after receiving her husband's last letter? Can you imagine how José's mother felt upon rereading this beautiful poem from her beloved son? Of course they were sad and devastated, but what a priceless gift! These two women had a loving, lasting legacy from their cherished loved ones to read and reread for the rest of their lives. Please, if you cannot bring yourself to express your deep feelings out loud to those you love, do so in writing. Your letter or poem will undoubtedly be passed on to future generations, who will feel the love and benefit from the warmth and sincerity of your genuine feelings.

> *All writing comes by the grace of God.*
>
> —RALPH WALDO EMERSON

Unconditional love

No book or chapter that I will ever write would be complete without a section devoted to our pets and the unconditional love they offer us, usually without expectation on their part of much in return.

I believe that I was born an animal lover. One of my primary recollections from first grade was crying copious tears over a sad dog story. But I never was allowed to have a dog as a child.

As a young bride, my first acquisition was a dog, of course. Somehow I cannot remember the puppy's name, but I can see him in my mind. Then there was Mickey, who came to us in Tucson, Arizona, and accompanied us to various air-force bases, including Nome, Alaska. Both he and my pilot husband, Campbell, died in Maine.

My next canine love was JB, for Jazz and Blues, named for the format of our radio station in Berkeley. JB lived at the station and woe unto any employee or prospective employee who was not a dog lover! Some companies encourage employees to bring their children to work; we encouraged employees to bring their dogs.

JB was hit by a car on his way to see his lady love a few blocks from the radio station; we, and many of our listeners, went into mourning for a week.

I understand that anywhere from 87 to 99 percent of dog owners see their canines as family members. How could they possibly think otherwise? My Charlie is not only my best friend and confidant, he is also my guardian. Yes, because he is basically a loud barker and therefore a great guard dog, I have anointed him with the title Guardian Angel Dog. That came from a night when I was quite distraught. I beseeched God to provide me with a guardian angel, someone in whom I could confide, who would console me when I was sad or in need. Charlie was lying on the floor beside my bed. After my prayer, he jumped on the bed and looked into my eyes. The message from God was, "Alice, you've always had a guardian dog in your loving Charlie." Since then, I have always felt calm, serene, and secure in the company of my dear, beloved Charlie.

I've said it before, and I think it bears repetition: Dogs share most of our positive emotions, but few of our negative ones, like spite, jealousy, vanity, hypocrisy, and bitterness. In addition, they're almost always in a good mood, ready to play at a moment's notice. Best of all, dogs give love, even when it is unrequited. No other animal loves us more than the dog, and there is probably no other friendship deeper than that between dogs and humans.

I love cats, too, but we all know they have their own agendas. I have one indoor cat, PK, and, currently, five or six members of the Breakfast Club, made up of my neighbor's outdoor cats. They are fun and amazing to watch because they all have individual personalities, but they are quite unlike dogs.

Regardless of what kind of pet you bring into your life and home, you will benefit from the closeness and experience. Pets help develop the concept of responsibility in children; they enrich a child's life and buffer critical situations for the young. But the most consistent benefits of pet ownership appear to be those realized by seniors. Companion animals help overcome loneliness while contributing to life's positive satisfactions; and seniors who have pets make fewer trips to the doctor and report fewer health complaints. For people of all ages, pets offer a source of emotional peace.

Yes, pets offer us so much in so many ways. But what might a pet have to say to us if it could speak? Beth Norman Harris offers her thoughts on what's on a dog's mind in this moving piece clipped from a Dear Abby column:

A DOG'S PRAYER
by Beth Norman Harris

Treat me kindly, my beloved master, for no heart in all the world is more grateful for kindness than the loving heart of me.

Do not break my spirit with a stick, for though I should lick your hand between the blows, your patience and understanding will more quickly teach me the things you would have me do.

Speak to me often, for your voice is the world's sweetest music, as you must know by the fierce wagging of my tail when your footstep falls upon my waiting ear.

Keep my pan filled with fresh water, for although I should not reproach you were it dry, I cannot tell you when I suffer thirst. Feed me clean food, that I may stay well, to romp and play and do your bidding, to walk by your side, and stand ready, willing and able to protect you with my life, should your life be in danger.

And, beloved master, should the Great Master see fit to deprive me of my health or sight, do not turn me away from you. Rather hold me gently in your arms as skilled hands grant me the merciful boon of eternal rest—and I will leave you knowing with the last breath I drew, my fate was ever safest in your hands.

There is something about the unselfish and self-sacrificing love of a brute, which goes directly to the heart of him who has had frequent occasions to test the paltry friendship and gossamer fidelity of mere man.

—EDGAR ALLAN POE

According to John 13:34, "A new commandment I give unto you, that you love one another." Please do so; love your family members, your neighbors, those in your community, your country, the world, the universe. And don't forget to love yourself, for that is where love begins. Start now, today, this minute.

My Resolutions

In regard to Commandment IX, *Love One Another,* these are my resolutions:

....
....
....
....
....
....
....
....
....
....
....
....
....
....
....
....
....
....
....
....
....
....

Have Fun—Enjoy—Live Life to the Fullest

I finally figured out the only reason to be alive is to enjoy it.

—RITA MAE BROWN

I have a friend whom I call the Philosopher of Fun. Actually, his name is Ray, but he tells me, in a serious tone, that "Fun" is his middle name. We were talking over lunch about the premise of this Commandment, and Ray said, "First of all, you've got to make a list!" To illustrate, he turned over the paper menu we were perusing and started to write. "You must put 'FUN' in capital letters at the very top of your list," instructed Ray as he wrote. "It's important to put fun at the very *top* of the list because it's the most important thing *on* your list. Then you must intersperse 'FUN' *throughout* your list." He proceeded to jot down a number of things that might be on a daily list, inserting "fun" throughout. "If you don't actually *write* in the word 'fun,' how are you going to remember to *have* fun?" Good question.

"Fun is something you have to look for regularly everywhere you go," continued Ray. "It's like bread pudding." "Bread pudding?" I asked. "What does bread pudding have to do with fun?" "It's the raisins," explained Ray. "Raisins are tucked in here and there in the pudding, you have to search them out. Raisins, like fun, become your tasty reward for the search." Not being especially fond of bread pudding or raisins, I asked, "Oh, you mean like bits of chocolate in chocolate-chip cookies?" Chocolate-chip cookies are more to my liking. "Yeah, you've got the idea," exclaimed a pleased Ray. "You've got to search for the chocolate chips, or raisins, in life. You've got to actively look for fun!"

> *Fun is fun but no girl wants to laugh all of the time.*
>
> —ANITA LOOS, *Gentleman Prefer Blondes*

My friend Allen Klein and I also talked about fun and where to find it. Allen, too, said you have to look for fun; in his analogy, he equated pennies with fun; looking at the bright side of life. At my request, Allen sent me this piece he wrote entitled "Pennies From Heaven."

There it is lying facedown on the sidewalk, slightly battered, frequently trampled upon and often ignored.

Pick it up or discard it?

Many people leave it lie there. I, on the other hand, get a sudden rush of excitement when I find one on the street ... just a penny. A seemingly worthless coin suddenly brings back memories that are pure gold. When I find a penny, my head starts humming a song I once heard in a Broadway show. It was about penny candy. I don't remember the exact lyrics but it was something about asking for more than a penny now because they are older and wiser.

I was a teenager when that show first opened; and yes, I've grown wiser and frequently want more than a penny now, but I am amazed how much pleasure I can still get from a one-cent coin.

I know a penny doesn't buy much these days. In fact, I'm not sure I can walk into any store and get anything for one single cent.

When I was growing up, however, it was pure joy to have a penny. I'd race to the candy store and immediately spend it. I could, looking back, even spend it without going inside. Every candy store in the neighborhood had a couple of machines outside where you could deposit your penny and walk away with either a handful of pistachio or pine nuts.

If I bypassed the nut machines and went directly into the candy store, I had a choice of spending my penny on such treats as red licorice ropes, dots of multicolored candy studded on a yard-long piece of paper (my favorite), or wax bottles filled with sugary syrup.

In spite of the high rate of inflation these days, and the fact that I can't even get one pistachio nut or a single licorice drop for a penny, street pennies still thrill me.

I recently read that $60 million worth of pennies are lost each year. I know, I find lots of them. Last year alone, I found twelve dollars and sixty-eight cents, mostly in pennies. (That averages out to nearly 3.5 cents a day or three and a half trips to the candy store in days past.)

I wonder why people don't pick up pennies nowadays. Has the value of a penny become so deflated that it is more trouble to bend down to retrieve them than they are worth?

Maybe the pleasure that I get from what others ignore stems from my father telling me that found money was "something special"; it was lucky when saved, unlucky when spent.

My father would stash away every bit of currency he found in a small antique desk clock. The money was frequently counted but never spent. And his "found money" is still cherished; I recently asked him for the clock, which he gladly gave, but the contents, of course, were removed. Maybe my reverence for copper coins comes, on the other hand, out of an incident that happened with my wife many years ago.

We were compatible in every way except one— money. I would get upset because I wanted to save it and she wanted to spend it. During one of our heated money-related arguments, we were walking in the park. I was complaining about her spending too much money and she was trying to convince me, in words not unlike those of Dolly Levi of *The Matchmaker* (and later *Hello, Dolly!*) that, "Money is like manure, you've got to spread it around and help young things grow." My wife's ideas about money were totally different from my notion of saving it in the bank and watching it grow that way.

No end of talking could convince me of my wife's viewpoint until I looked down and there I saw not one but several pennies at my feet. We both laughed as she reminded me that God always provides and always will. And she was right.

The coins I find on the street not only remind me

of the joyful memories from the past, but perhaps more importantly, they are little lessons which teach me to be thankful for the abundance in my life, no matter how small.

Thank you, Allen, for reminding us to look for the pennies, as well as the raisins, in our daily lives. I, too, feel a surge of exhilaration when I find a penny on the street. I always pick it up; to me it means something good is going to happen. I have quite a stash of found pennies, but unlike Allen, I don't average 3.5 cents a day. Perhaps I'm treading the wrong streets.

> *A penny saved is a penny earned.*
>
> —Old saying

It is doubtful that picking up pennies will make you wealthy. You'd be wiser to look to your parents for that, says Art, my new friend. "It's easy to *inherit* money, but you must *earn* respect." And Art's entire life has been built on the premise of earning respect. Along the way, he has accumulated most of the good things we all strive for, and he enjoys those material things. But Art has had a great deal of fun along the way as well, and he continues to produce fun and good times in his life, which makes him a most interesting, enjoyable person to be with.

In his early seventies, well past retirement age, Art continues to work—and that word should be in quotes, because, to Art, work is play, and it always has been. Art is a real-estate developer; every deal is a challenge, and he's swung some big ones. The adrenaline rush that comes from putting it all together and negotiating the final contract is stimulating beyond measure, according to Art. Then, to watch the shopping center or housing development materialize and become a reality—is there anything sweeter? he wonders. All work and no play? To Art, all work *is* play!

Yes, Art has his fun side. He loves to dress in his western attire, complete with cowboy boots and Stetson, and, with guitar in tow, sing to an appreciative audience of country-music lovers. "Fun?" asks Art. "I have more fun than a dozen other people. To me, every day is better than yesterday. In fact, *any* day I see is a good day." He felt obliged to elaborate by saying, "Any day *above-ground* is a good day!" Agreed.

> *Resolved: To live with all my might while I do live, and as I shall wish I had done ten thousand ages hence.*
>
> —JONATHAN EDWARDS

While Art loves to work, Mary cautions, "Don't work too much. I'm guilty of this, obviously, because I find I'm happier when I'm busy. Also, it keeps me going. But we all need to take time to get away occasionally, even if for only a long weekend. You've got to make time for enjoyment. Sometimes, just taking time to have lunch with a friend is wonderful."

Taking time with your grandchildren can also be wonderful. So said my friend Rose when I asked her what fun means to her. "Doing things with the kids, Darius and Asia, that's my fun. They love trains, so we go to Jack London Square a lot to watch the trains.

There's a train in Tilden Park, too. The kids love going there, because in addition to the train, there's a merry-go-round and horses. Best of all, there are no cars in the park, so I don't have to worry about traffic.

"One of the things that gives my grandkids the biggest kick is when we play games and reverse roles. They become Grandma or Grandpa, and I revert to becoming the child. It's truly amazing what comes out of these sessions! It's amusing how they relate to me in our reverse roles; they bawl me out if, according to them, I misbehave. Very interesting—it really keeps me on my toes as I get to see things from their perspective."

To Craig, fun is more literal; fun is something that makes you laugh out loud. And that usually has something to do with a prank or joke, the April Fools' Day kind of thing. When I looked surprised, he assured me that his practical jokes never hurt anyone, they were just—well, just fun!

For example, there was the time when he worked for a software company and was able to reproduce authentic-looking parking tickets. The company had a huge parking lot, which was usually completely filled with cars. One April Fools' Day, Craig snuck out and put his bogus parking tickets on a significant number of cars during lunch hour. The recipients of the tickets took them for the real thing, and you can imagine the uproar that ensued. It wasn't until they examined the tickets closely and read their supposed misdemeanors that they got the joke. Craig's ticket cited them for such things as "excessive use of farce" and "impersonating a manager."

Another time, Craig relates, the employees held a surprise birthday party for a coworker—or at least they started the party—in the company's men's room! He also told me of a "holiday" that he calls "Mental Pause Day," which is traditionally observed on June 30th. I've never heard of it, but it sure sounds like a good idea. Craig's advice: "When you play hooky on Mental Pause Day and go to a ball game, don't get caught on TV. And if you go to the beach, don't get a sunburn. Both are sure giveaways that you've been goofing off."

> *No man who has once heartily and wholly laughed can be altogether irreclaimably bad.*
>
> —THOMAS CARLYLE

A happy attitude makes all the difference

Recently, I went to a Nordstrom store in a nearby suburban shopping center to exchange a pair of boots. The shoe department was packed, a total madhouse, as usual. Despairing of ever being waited on, I sat down next to a pleasant-looking woman and decided to wait until her salesperson was free. The woman and I started chatting and I soon discovered that she used to live near my home in Oakland, and we discussed the changes in the neighborhood. In between, the young woman waiting on her, and then me, joined in the parts of the conversation that touched upon life, living, and enjoying.

I was quite taken with the upbeat, friendly attitude of the young salesclerk, who, given the hordes of people asking for assistance, should have been harried and stressed-out. Instead, she was calm, serene, and helpful; her smile never left her face. "I love my job," she told me when I asked about her positive attitude. "What would I accomplish by getting stressed-out? I had heart surgery four months ago, and I'm happy to be alive. I'm just thirty-two, and I realize I have my whole life ahead of me. I simply will not allow anyone or anything to depress me or put me in a burnout position. As someone once said, 'It's almost impossible to smile on the outside without feeling better on the inside."

I asked for her card, and learned that her name was Juli. I wrote to Juli about a week later and asked if she would contact me so we could talk further about her remarkable positive attitude. When she called, we only had moments to chat because she was rushing to work, but she told me all I needed to know. Actually, she told me what I know and have always known. "It's all a state of mind, Alice," she said. "Your life is determined by the way you think. I only think happy thoughts, therefore I'm happy. I was married for a time to the most negative guy you could ever meet; being with him was totally depressing, but I didn't realize that at the time. When we divorced, and I got away from that oppressive mind-set, it was a revelation! I felt that I was finally free. I think that the time we spent together contributed to my illness, but now that is all behind me. I am happy to be alive. I enjoy every moment of every day. Because of my happy attitude, my sales are going through the roof. Life is wonderful and I intend to live it to the hilt! I now have a new boyfriend; we're planning our future together and life is totally beautiful."

> *Live all you can; it's a mistake not to. It doesn't so much matter what you do in particular, so long as you have your life. If you haven't had that, what have you had?*
>
> **—HENRY JAMES**

Fun is everywhere

Ray, my Philosopher of Fun, says you've got to look for fun and unexpected surprises everywhere. One of his favorite leisure activities is what he calls "green spotting." This requires a local map; he suggests going to your nearby AAA, or equivalent, and picking up a selection of area maps. Then, according to Ray, you look for the green spots. The green spots are local parks. Pick out a small one, they're the most friendly, promises Ray, and less likely to have crowds of people. Go on off days, not on the weekend, and take a picnic basket and a bottle of wine. Green spotting. Try it! You'll have fun!

Ray is also all in favor of freebies, two-for-one offers, and special deals. He suggested that I look for two-for-one restaurant offers in the local neighborhood newspaper and in the coupons that come in the mail, and then use them. Why stay home when you can dine out for half price? The day we discussed all of this over lunch, we enjoyed free corkage at the restaurant we chose, something quite unusual in this neck of the woods. As Ray pointed out, there's lots around us to be thankful for and, sometimes, the best things in life are free—or at least relatively inexpensive.

Mary echoed that thought. "There is much to be thankful for. Daily, count your blessings. And," she continued, "be sure to give something back to some worthy cause, whatever is closest to you. Maybe it's your church, or some other cause you're interested in. But do give something back." Mary is an exemplary person, a true example of doing unto others and living life to the fullest.

When faced with a freight train or other delay, count your blessings

Recently, my son, Mark, and four-year-old grandson, Campbell, arrived to take me out to lunch. We decided to go to a restaurant in Jack London Square, which is located on Oakland's estuary, so that Campbell could watch the boats and other water activity while having lunch. On our way, we were stopped by a very long freight train, a daily occurrence on the outskirts of Jack London Square, causing me to fume over the delay. The train did not bother Mark and Campbell in the least. In fact, they were thrilled at the opportunity to watch the various cars go slowly by and speculate about what might be contained within each one, and its eventual destination.

"Have you been counting the cars, Campbell? How many do you suppose there are there on this train?" Mark asked his son. "Oh, Daddy! There are too many. I can't count *that* high!" Campbell laughed. Then it occurred to me that rather than fuming over the fifteen-minute delay caused by the inevitable freight train, I could have spent the time, not in counting the cars or wondering about their content and possible destinations, but in counting something far more important, something that would contribute greatly to my appreciation of the day. I could have been counting my blessings, one blessing for each car that passed. And, like Campbell, I would have found that there are too many to count.

To be happy is easy enough if we give ourselves, forgive others, and live with thanksgiving. No self-centered person, no ungrateful soul can ever be happy, much less make anyone else happy. Life is giving, not getting.

—JOSEPH FORT NEWTON

My friend Allen the Jollytologist is an expert on living with joy. He should be, as he speaks and writes on the subject of humor. Allen is on the road much of the time, and consequently is not always able to celebrate special occasions with his friends and family at home. He sent me this piece, which explains his solution to that problem:

HAPPY MIRTHDAY
By Allen Klein

For the past three years, every time it was my birthday, I have either been out of town because I was attending a conference or presenting one of my own humor programs. This past year, I was once again not pleased to have to spend my birthday in an unfamiliar city with a group of strangers who had no inkling that it was a special time for me. So I decided to change all that. Before I left town, I was determined to create an outrageously fun birthday for myself in spite of the fact that I was far from home.

The first thing I did was to let everyone I came in contact with at the conference I was attending know that it was my birthday. Then I told them that I wanted a hug from each of them. I not only got hugs throughout the day but throughout the conference as well.

Later on in the day, in a crowded elevator, I announced my birthday and asked twelve total strangers to sing "Happy Birthday" as I exited. What a wonderfully funny sight seeing an elevator filled with adults singing "Happy birthday to you . . ." as the doors were closing. Next, I bought some flowers for myself. After I selected a stem of lilies, I asked the florist if she had a birthday card to include with my selection. She handed me one, and then noticing how much time and thought I was taking in writing the card, she asked, "Oh, are you buying for someone special?" "Yes," I said. "Me." She looked puzzled and then laughed as I wrote, "To Allen. Happy Birthday. I love you." And then I signed my name.

What I noticed throughout the day was that everyone I told that it was my birthday, from the hassled hotel desk clerk who gave me a bud vase for my flowers to the convenience-store clerk who looked like she hadn't smiled in years, not only willingly participated in my offbeat requests but, without an exception, immediately smiled, became friendly, and a most willing participant to help me celebrate my special day.

Then it struck me: I had just discovered "The Mirthday Phenomenon." Tell someone it's your birthday, whether it actually is or not, and suddenly they cheer up.

So, the next time you are down when out of town (or even in town for that matter), tell some-

*one (or everyone) it's your birthday (even if it
isn't)—and you'll create a Happy Mirthday too.*

Right on, Allen! I am all for celebrating birthdays, both
mine and those of friends and relatives. And the longer
you can stretch out the festivities—some manage to
make them span a number of weeks—the better. Just
think how dull your year would be if you didn't have a
special day of your very own in which to be indulged.
And if, like Allen, the situation requires that you do the
indulging, so what? The point is to have fun on your
birthday!

*How old would you be if you didn't know how
old you was?*

—SATCHEL PAIGE

Enjoying life—it's an inside job

I asked Paul, my wise, longtime correspondent, for
his thoughts on the theme of this Commandment. Paul
responded as follows:

*Live life to the fullest, a wonderful commandment!
What does it really mean? What is enjoyment?
What is fun? All-important questions, and not so
easily answered. We all are not born with the
same aptitudes. Society all too often expects everyone to be measured by the same yardstick. At some
point in life we all realize, or should, that joy, fun,
happiness, and fulfillment really do come from the
inner corners of one's own mind.*

I love to create, be inventive, and experiment

in different directions, all in photography. I do have the will and attitude of an artist, but after that wish is realized and one works hard to refine one's skill, what then?

Photography is my passion and I fully believe that we all experience at least one passion in our lives. It's that feeling of being driven to do something which, in the end, really makes life pleasurable and rewarding. But some people excel at a myriad of activities. Are these people getting more fun out of life than someone who simply concentrates on one field of endeavor? Good question!

The problem, as I see it, is that one must embark on pursuits which give one that inner lift, as it were, without any thought about where it might end. Will my hobby become a career? for example. When one focuses on the doing of something and not actually on the outcome, to sort of lose oneself in the moment and passion of doing, the feeling of consummation can be far more rewarding, to my way of thinking. Living life to the fullest, to me, means a collection of moments all put together in such a way that we can build on each past snippet of fun and enjoyment to create a sense of fullness of self.

In my opinion, childhood is the key. I had a blast in my younger years. Spending three years in rural New Hampshire when I was six, seven, and eight set the entire tone for me. I learned many things in those three years. I learned about nature and how to sit quietly and watch and listen to it. I learned how to keep warm in the winter and stay off the ice in the springtime. I learned how not to get lost in the woods at age seven.

Those early experiences created the aura that surrounds me in later life. I can feel down in the dumps and go hiking at Point Reyes and become renewed again. Photography is simply a means for me to recreate what I'm feeling inside about places, people, or things.

There is always one moment in childhood when the door opens and lets the future in.

—GRAHAM GREENE

Look to the past for future fun

If you're looking for fun, and don't know where to find it, you might follow Paul's example and revert, temporarily, to childhood or to times past when having fun was an accepted part of daily life. Thinking about my fun times as a young girl, my recollection is that I enjoyed opposite activities: being with friends, laughing, talking, sharing, doing, even getting into mischief, and at other times, I thoroughly enjoyed being alone, reading. In analyzing myself, I find the same applies today. I enjoy being with friends, participating in and sharing experiences, activities, and ideas, and at other times, just being alone reading a book is what pleases me. Above all, being alone *writing* a book is what interests me most and consumes me totally. I hope this is evident to those who might eventually read my books.

Pen pal Bob, in his most recent letter, had this to say about Commandment X:

It has been said that fun is where you find it. And I guess finding it to a large extent is a matter of

*seeking. Some people never have any fun, proba-
bly because they don't really want to, feeling as if
they don't deserve it, or it might disturb some pre-
vailing negative mind-set which demands a sour
outlook on life. I recall reading that an inability
to experience pleasure can be a symptom of clin-
ical depression, at least in some cases.*

*In my own life, I have, if anything, been much
too interested in having a good time, with not
enough focus on activities which, though necessary, are not particularly enjoyable and are sometimes downright tedious. Of course, enjoyability or
tediousness are like beauty: they're in the eye of
the beholder. Certainly, many regard reading as
tedious and will do it only under the prod of necessity, whereas I personally put reading near the
top of my list of enjoyable activities.*

*People say that life is the thing, but I prefer
reading.*

—LOGAN PEARSALL SMITH

Being calm and peaceful is a personal choice

Yesterday morning I set my alarm to awaken me for
an early-morning interview with John St. Augustine on
Power Talk Radio, WDBC, in upstate Michigan. Because of the three-hour time difference between California and Michigan, I had to be awake and sounding
chipper before it was barely light at my end. This was
my third on-air conversation with John on the subject of
positive thinking in general, and my three books in par-

ticular. While on the air, Pat, a regular listener, called in and said she had a question for me. "This is the third time I've heard you talk with John," said Pat, "and you always sound so calm and peaceful. What is your secret?"

Me, calm and peaceful? I was surprised that, caught in the middle of my personal soap opera, I was able to exude those attributes. But I was pleased with Pat's assessment of my state of mind, or outlook, and I endeavored to answer her with total honestly.

"It's a matter of attitude, Pat," I told her. "It's all in the way you look at life. Whether you're happy or sad, whether you enjoy life or find it tedious, depends on your individual outlook." I went on to tell her that I count my blessings every night before I go to sleep. I don't have to get far into my list of blessings before any complaints I might have dissolve. I realize how fortunate I am to be me and to be able to do the things I enjoy most. I do not envy anyone. I told her that I am especially grateful that I am able to write books, because doing so gives me great pleasure and is personally rewarding beyond measure.

Enjoying life is a choice, as are so many other things. You have to make up your mind to enjoy. It doesn't mean that I or others who enjoy are more gifted or fortunate than those who choose to see the half-empty glass or the doughnut hole. It does mean that we simply decide; we *choose* to be happy, to enjoy, to be calm, to be peaceful. Our attitude toward life becomes a self-fulfilling prophesy; if we choose to be happy, to enjoy, that's what we get out of life: happiness and enjoyment. If we decide that life is difficult and depressing, that's what we get: a difficult and depressing life.

*Happiness is an attitude. We either make our-
selves miserable, or happy and strong. The
amount of work is the same.*

—FRANCESCA REIGLER

Happiness and enjoyment come from doing, from being
passionately involved in something that is meaningful to
you. Rather than looking, searching for such intangibles
as happiness and enjoyment, look for that something that
turns you on. Become involved. Live life. Happiness and
enjoyment become natural by-products of living your
personal passion.

*If you observe a really happy man, you will find
him building a boat, writing a symphony, edu-
cating his son, growing double dahlias or looking for dinosaur eggs in the Gobi Desert. He will
not be searching for happiness as if it were a
collar button that had rolled under the radia-
tor, striving for it as a goal in itself. He will have
become aware that he is happy in the course of
living life twenty-four crowded hours of each
day.*

—W. BERAN WOLFE

Live life to the fullest

Live life to the fullest. What does that mean? To me
it means a lot of things. It means living today as if there
were no tomorrow. It means not putting off things you
really want to do until a better time; there may never be
a better time. It means writing that loving letter, phoning

those who are special in your life to tell them how much they mean to you, sending thank-you notes, not only for gifts, but for favors you appreciate, asking if you can help a friend who may be having a difficult time, running an errand for a neighbor, listening to someone who needs a shoulder to cry on. It means being available, appreciative, giving, and thankful. It means extending yourself beyond your comfort zone for others once in a while; you may be in a position to need the same from them one day.

Do unto others as you would have others do unto you.

—MATTHEW 7:12

It means living life with as few regrets as possible. This can be explained succinctly by one of my all-time favorite quotes, which I've shared with you before earlier in this book. But because it is so very appropriate to this thought, I'll repeat it here:

Regret for the things we did can be tempered by time; it is regret for the things we did not do that is inconsolable.

—SYDNEY J. HARRIS

Forget the past with its disappointments and worries. The past is dead and gone. The present is *it*, your future in the making. As someone said, "Do it now! Today will be yesterday tomorrow." Forgive yesterday's regrets. Be concerned with today and your dreams and goals. If you do not do it now, you may never do it, whatever it is.

And you will be inconsolable. If you are "dying" to do something, heed these words:

> *First I was dying to finish high school and start college. And then I was dying to finish college and start working. And then I was dying to marry and have children. And then I was dying for my children to grow old enough so I could return to work. And then I was dying to retire. And now, I am dying—and suddenly realize I forgot to live.*
>
> —ANONYMOUS

How many of us can relate to that? Please, do not put your life on hold for the future. *Do not forget to live!* And don't worry about the inevitable mistakes that go along with living.

> *If I had my life to live over again, I'd try to make more mistakes next time—would relax. I'd be sillier than I have been on this trip. I would climb more mountains, swim more rivers and watch more sunsets. I would have more actual troubles and less imaginary ones. Oh, I've had my moments, and if I had to do it over again, I'd have more of them. In fact, I'd try to have nothing else, just moments, one after another— I would pick more daisies.*
>
> —NADINE STAIR, at age eight-nine

After I typed that wonderful piece, I started to think of all the things I'd do if I had my life to live over again. A wonderful exercise, and one that I recommend for you. So, take time out right now and write your "If I had my life to live over again" list. Note that this list incorporates everything in life *up to now*. Unfortunately, because of the passage of time and the passing of people, many of the things on this list cannot be or be done or accomplished. Not all, but many.

Now look at your list. Of all the things you wrote, what can you *still* do now, today? This week? Next week? Next month? Before the year is over? Please, do all of the things on your "up to now" list if you possibly can.

Next, get another piece of paper and start another list. This is your "from now on" list. This list is more important than your "up to now" list because the latter is essentially an "if only" list, a wishful thinking list, a reliving the past list. Your "from now on" list is a positive list, one that you start working on today, one that can, and should, be achieved if you are serious about living life to the fullest.

> *You don't get to choose how you're going to die. Or when. You can only decide how you're going to live. Now.*
>
> —JOAN BAEZ

Have fun—enjoy—live life to the fullest. This is your *raison d'être*! Remember, it is God's will that we enjoy all of the good things He has provided us. If being able to enjoy does not come to us naturally because, perhaps, we think we're not entitled, we must learn to *cultivate* the art of enjoying. If for no other reason, we must enjoy because it's good for our health.

A cheerful heart is a good medicine, but a downcast spirit dries up the bones.

—PROVERBS 17:22

Have fun—enjoy—live life to the fullest. This is your final Commandment.

Everyone will be called to account on Judgment Day for all the legitimate pleasures which he or she has failed to enjoy.

—TALMUD

My Resolutions

In regard to Commandment X, *Have Fun—Enjoy— Live Life to the Fullest,* these are my resolutions:

....
....
....
....
....
....
....
....
....
....
....
....
....
....
....
....
....
....
....
....
....
....
....
....

Oakland, California
July 9, 1999

A personal note to you, my readers:

The genesis of this Book of Commandments began before I can even remember; the writing of it well over a year ago.

In this, as in everything I've ever written, I feel as if I am speaking to you, personally, on a one-to-one basis. In my mind, I talk and relate to you as if we were family, longtime friends, or neighbors.

When I come to the end of a manuscript, I feel sad, adrift, lost even—because, to me, we've become so close, I cannot imagine saying good-bye.

Please know that I welcome and encourage your thoughts and comments in regard to this, or any of my previous books.

I want to know about you and how you are doing in this adventure we call life.

Do write to me, if you care to. I will respond. Here is my address:

Alice Potter
P.O. Box 10096
Oakland, CA 94610

Thank you.

Fondly,

Alice

More positive thoughts from
Alice Potter...

Putting the Positive Thinker to Work

Positive thinking is only the beginning...Once you've learned to let yourself dream, to see the bright side in yourself and others, and to believe that the best is yet to come--it's time to make that future happen! With this upbeat guide, the author of *The Positive Thinker* shows you how, with simple, solid ways to take charge of your life, to let go of last-minute jitters...and make yourself happy.

❑ 0-425-16376-8/$6.50